The Teaching Assistant's Guide

This indispensable new textbook, designed specifically to meet the needs of students on the Teaching Assistant Foundation Degree course, provides a sorely needed and highly accessible overview of the modern Teaching Assistant's role.

Packed full of comprehensive yet thoroughly grounded advice and practical tasks, this book includes sections covering all the different ideas, situations and problems that a Teaching Assistant can expect to encounter, including:

- Personal professional development – helping Teaching Assistants to understand their role and workplace.
- Growth, development and learning – introducing the basic theories of human development and learning.
- Behaviour management – exploring strategies that encourage and support appropriate behaviour.
- Today's curriculum – how learning takes place in literacy, mathematics, science and technology.
- Understanding inclusive education – exploring access, participation and additional needs for specific groups of young people.

With activities, task lists, discussion points, ideas, summary points and notes on further reading, this textbook will be *the* essential companion for all Foundation Degree students. It will also be invaluable reading for NVQ students and practising Teaching Assistants, as well as those who teach or manage them.

Linda Hammersley-Fletcher is Senior Lecturer and Researcher at Staffordshire University, UK. Before completing her teacher training and PhD she was a Teaching Assistant in both the primary and secondary sectors.

Michelle Lowe leads the Foundation Degree for Teaching Assistants at Staffordshire University, UK. She has extensive experience of working across the primary sector at a senior level.

Jim Pugh is Lecturer and Course Team Leader within the Teacher Education Department at Stoke-on-Trent College. He has worked across several educational sectors during his career, and still teaches in primary schools.

Related titles from Routledge:

A Teaching Assistant's Guide to Managing Behaviour in the Classroom
Susan Bentham
0–415–35119–7

A Teaching Assistant's Guide to Primary Education
Joan Dean
0–415–35234–7

Practical Tips for Teaching Assistants
Susan Bentham
0–415–35472–2

A Teaching Assistant's Guide to Child Development and Psychology in the Classroom
Susan Bentham
0–415–31107–1 (hb) / 0–415–31108–X (pb)

The Teaching Assistant's Guide

An essential textbook for foundation degree students

Linda Hammersley-Fletcher,
Michelle Lowe and Jim Pugh

Routledge
Taylor & Francis Group

LONDON AND NEW YORK

First published 2006
by Routledge
2 Park Square, Milton Park, Abingdon, Oxon OX14 4RN

Simultaneously published in the USA and Canada
by Routledge
270 Madison Ave, New York, NY 10016

Routledge is an imprint of the Taylor & Francis Group, an informa business

Transferred to Digital Printing 2009

Typeset in Goudy by
HWA Text and Data Management, Tunbridge Wells

British Library Cataloguing in Publication Data
A catalogue record for this book is available from the British Library

Library of Congress Cataloging-in-Publication Data
Hammersley-Fletcher, Linda.
The teaching assistant's guide : an essential textbook for foundation
degree students / Linda Hammersley-Fletcher, Michelle Lowe and
Jim Pugh.– 1st ed.
   p. cm.
Includes bibliographical references and index.
1. Teachers' assistants. 2. Teachers' assistants–Handbooks, manuals, etc.
I. Lowe, Michelle, 1963– II. Pugh, Jim 1976– III. Title.
LB2844.1.A8H36 2006
378.1'2–dc22   200503925

ISBN10: 0–415–34568–5 (pbk)
ISBN10: 0–203–56718–8 (ebk)

ISBN13: 978–0–415–34568–2 (pbk)
ISBN13: 978–0–203–56718–0 (ebk)

Contents

List of figures   vi
Dedication and acknowledgements   vii

1 An overview of this book   1

2 Personal and professional development and the role of the
   Teaching Assistant   9

3 Growth, development and learning   21

4 The development of language and literacy   42

5 Numeracy   61

6 Science   74

7 Information and communication technology (ICT)   86

8 Behaviour management   97

9 Inclusive education   111

10 Child protection   122

11 Planning and assessment   130

12 The Teaching Assistant and concepts in education   142

   Appendix I: record of task progress   158
   Index   162

Figures

2.1	The 25 Tasks	13
2.2	Working with Teaching Assistants	16
2.3	The National Qualification Framework	19
3.1	Piaget's stages of development	25
3.2	The learning cycle	29
3.3	Kagan and Lang: major motives and desires	30
3.4	Maslow's Hierarchy of Needs	31
4.1	Transmission and interpretation models	44
4.2	A bottom-up model	49
4.3	A top-down model	50
4.4	Writing as a continuum	52
4.5	The writing process	53
4.6	The effect of modelling upon performance	56
5.1	The development of the mathematics curriculum	63
5.2	Outline of a Daily Mathematics Lesson	65
5.3	Inclusion of whole-class interactive teaching in the Daily Mathematics Lesson	65
5.4	Ways of resolving misconceptions	69
6.1	Interaction within conceptual understanding	76
6.2	Piaget's conceptualisation of schemas	77
6.3	Scientific vocabulary	81
7.1	Paradigms of learning and computers	88
7.2	Ways of differentiating	95
8.1	Progressive warnings	107
9.1	History of SEN	113
9.2	Graduated approach to process SEN children	117
11.1	The cyclical nature of planning and assessment	133
12.1	Strategic drift and economic and social change	144
12.2	A sequence for moral development	153
12.3	Kohlberg's stage of cognitive development	153
12.4	Key features of each stage of learning	155

Dedication and acknowledgements

We would like to dedicate this book to all the hardworking and unsung heroes and heroines of the classroom – the TAs.

We would also like to thank our families, friends and colleagues for their continuing support and patience.

Chapter 1

An overview of this book

This book is designed to support Teaching Assistants both in their role within the workplace and during study for qualifications such as a Foundation Degree. Thus it has both practical and academic elements. Each chapter will explore the development of skills and the ways in which the Teaching Assistant can support learners.

Introduction

Working in educational settings and studying for a higher qualification both involve Teaching Assistants (TAs) in the consideration of concepts and theories of child development, teaching and learning and working with young learners. This book is intended to supply you with a broad basis for that study. It will help you to answer the questions about how and why, and give you the underpinning knowledge that you may need for further study. In this introduction we explain how the book is structured and give you an overview of the contents. We also offer some practical advice and suggestions to support the development of your academic skills.

As authors we realise that Teaching Assistants come from a variety of backgrounds and consequently have tried to make the text accessible to all whilst providing stimulating challenges. Each chapter is structured to begin with an outline of the contents and to suggest tasks that will help re-enforce the particular concepts and theories being discussed. The tasks are varied, some requiring you to think about your own practice whereas others require a written response. You will find a task summary record in Appendix 1 which will help you to record your work. In addition, each chapter contains subheadings that will help you find the information you need quickly. There is a section at the end of each chapter which will provide you with some useful suggestions for further reading. This structure ensures that chapters may be read independently of one another and so you do not have to read this book from cover to cover. It is, however, helpful to read the introduction first in order to gain a full picture of what the book contains. The index will also help you find a reference to a particular point of interest.

In developing your study skills it is often helpful to begin by reading about the issue you are interested in so that you become familiar with the ideas presented. It is then a good idea to re-read this information making notes as you go. In reading this book you may also want to carry out the tasks that have been designed to help you structure your thinking about an issue in a way that relates it to your own practice.

What's in the book?

The book begins by exploring the role of the Teaching Assistant and provides you with a brief history of the development of the role, taking account of the legislative framework (Chapter 2). In Chapter 3 we introduce you to theories of child development and learning exploring how learners make sense of their world and what motivates them. We also introduce the concept of different forms of intelligence and outline the link between the physical development of the brain and the capacity to learn. The next four chapters look at learning in literacy, numeracy, science and information and communications technology (ICT). The literacy chapter addresses the acquisition of language and language development and considers the teaching of literacy, outlining the interrelationship between speaking, listening, reading and writing. The numeracy chapter introduces you to the development of the numeracy curriculum, the development of mathematical knowledge and understanding in learners, the teaching of numeracy and ways of supporting mathematics. The science chapter discusses ways of thinking about science and the theories of learning development that have been influential in relation to the science curriculum. It explores the structure of the science curriculum and examines the link between literacy skills and science. ICT has been identified as a discrete element within this book. ICT underpins the development of skills in many curriculum areas but it is also a subject in its own right within the curriculum. In this chapter we look at the reasons for including ICT in the curriculum, the curriculum content and provide examples for good practice.

Managing behaviour is an important skill for all those involved in education and in Chapter 8 we explore ways of managing the behaviour of all learners to achieve a positive outcome. Chapter 9 presents you with an overview of the development of the provision for learners with special educational needs and examines the concept of 'Inclusion'. It includes an overview of the current legislative framework and the ways in which organisations can meet the needs of all learners. Regretfully, many young people require protection from abuse. Educators have a key role to play in identifying those at risk and ensuring that the correct procedures are followed in relation to child protection. Therefore in Chapter 10 we outline the legislative framework and provide you with an overview exploring some forms of abuse. We also outline the key roles and responsibilities of staff in relation to child protection and in particular those related to the role of the Teaching Assistant. In Chapter 11 we look at planning and assessment. Whilst you may not be directly involved in planning it underpins the daily working life of the Teaching Assistant. We argue that Teaching Assistants need to be involved in planning for learning and that they should be aware of the importance of planning to ensure an effective learning environment. This chapter also outlines different forms of assessment, including e-learning. Finally Chapter 12 aims to encourage you to engage with fundamental questions concerning the aims and values of education and its relationship to society. It explores the problematic nature of educational theory, policy and practice and encourages the interrogation of education processes. It will help you to recognise the wider context within which education takes place through an exploration of the socio-economic and political influences on education policy and practice.

In this book we have used the generic term 'learner' throughout. However where the concept we have introduced applies specifically to an educational phase we have used the most appropriate term. For example, when we discuss the development of speech we refer to children and the child, whereas our discussions of the acquisition of reading refer to learners in acknowledgement of the fact that learning to read can happen at any age. Similarly, we have used the terms 'organisations' or 'workplaces' to encompass all the different educational settings where Teaching Assistants work. However, there are some concepts and polices that are sector specific. Where this is the case we have used the most common name; for example, when discussing remodelling we refer to 'schools' because remodelling has not yet been applied in post-16 contexts.

Study skills

The development of study skills is important whether you wish to study for a qualification or simply want to keep your knowledge and understanding up to date. Study can also take different forms, for example 'learning on the job'. As Teaching Assistants you may be collecting information for inclusion in a portfolio or been asked to write short accounts of what you do referenced against national standards. If you are studying for a University or College qualification you will be engaged with a different type of learning. Whilst you may be involved in a substantial element of work-based learning you are also required to complete a range of academic assignments (essays). Such assignments usually require you to consider particular concepts and theories and make an evaluation of these, often in relation to your own practice. For example, if you were writing an essay on literacy you may need to show that you understand how learners acquire language and make reference to the theory of other writers and then show how this is utilised in your workplace. In our experience as educators it is this academic writing that people find most worrying when beginning their studies, particularly if it is a long time since they last wrote anything academic. These skills can be quickly acquired, developed and improved with the help of some practical guidance.

Task 1A

Think about how you like to learn. Can you recall a time when you studied effectively and a time when your learning didn't go according to plan?
    Why do you think this happened?

How do you learn?

We each have a preferred learning style, a way of learning. This is often the way we learn best. We can identify three main learning styles:

➡ Auditory
➡ Visual
➡ Kinaesthetic

Are you an Auditory Learner?

Auditory Learners learn best when information is presented in a spoken format. For example, you may learn best in class with a teacher or lecturer explaining what you need to know and during class discussions. Does listening to audio tapes help you to learn better? Do you find yourself reading aloud or talking things out to gain better understanding? If you answered yes to these questions then you are likely to be an Auditory Learner.

Are you a Visual Learner?

Visual Learners learn best when information is presented to them in a written format. This could also include pictures or diagrams. You may learn best in classes where teachers do a lot of writing, provide clear handouts, and make use of an overhead projector. Do you try to remember information by creating pictures in your mind? Do you take written notes? If you answered yes to these questions then you are likely to be a Visual Learner.

Are you a Kinaesthetic Learner?

Kinaesthetic Learners learn best by doing. They prefer hands-on learning where they can physically manipulate something in order to learn about it. You might learn best when you can move about and handle things. If you do then you are likely to be a Kinaesthetic Learner.

You can use your preferred learning style to help you as a student. Simply choose study techniques that suit the way you learn.

Managing your study time

There are only so many hours in a day, a week, and a term so it is important to manage your study time carefully. You cannot change the number of hours in a day, but you can decide how to use them to achieve the maximum effect. Decide how many hours a week you need to spend on study and then secure that time for yourself. Some people like to spend several hours at a time working and so might choose to study on a Sunday afternoon, for example. Others might choose to do short bursts of study, say between 8 pm and 9.30 pm in the evening. In addition, you may find that you think better at a particular time of the day. For example, you may be a 'morning person' and feel it worthwhile getting up a little earlier and doing some work before the rush of the day begins. It can help to prepare a calendar on which you record various dates such as times when you will study, when assignments are due and any other scheduled tasks. This may help you to keep to your plan.

Somewhere to study

Remember that you need somewhere to study. It may be a corner of a room or bedroom. You may be lucky enough to have a spare room that you could use. Consider the following points when choosing somewhere to study.

➤➤ Is my study area available to me at the times that I need it?
➤➤ Is my study area free from interruptions and distractions?
➤➤ Does my study area have all of the study materials I need?

➤➤ Does my study area have a desk or table?
➤➤ Does my study area have storage space?
➤➤ Does my study area have a comfortable chair?
➤➤ Does my study area have enough light?
➤➤ Does my study area have a comfortable temperature?

Reading

It is very important that you read around any subject you are studying. For example each chapter in this book contains references to other books that provide helpful additional information. If you are studying for a qualification you will have reading lists provided. Many students make the mistake of thinking that they must read everything. It is up to you to choose what to read from these lists based on your interests, your study needs and the readability of the text. It is often helpful to look at the book in a library before buying it to ensure that it is exactly what you want. Of course you can read additional texts but it is important when studying to remain focussed on the needs of your course and not allow yourself to get too sidetracked by other interesting areas (and there are lots of them). Consider how relevant the book is to your study needs?

You will also need to allow time for reading. This can be difficult to find. It may be helpful to time yourself reading the first chapter of this book to give you an idea of how much time you will need. When you read you need to ask yourself some questions:

➤➤ Do you understand what the main points of the chapter/section are?
➤➤ Can you link what you are reading to your own experience or to other things you have read?
➤➤ Do you agree or disagree with the ideas – why?

It is important to realise that you do not have to agree with every point of view you read and the more you explore a particular issue the more you will discover a range of ideas about it from which you will need to decide which perspective you most sympathise with and why.

> Information on its own is nothing. Information only provides access to power when it is linked with reason and thought … people must make selections from it. To connect diverse strands of it together, to ask intelligent questions of it and to reject parts of it which, though they appear there on the screen, in the book or on the paper, appears inaccurate.
>
> (Barber 1996: 181)

Some people work best by reading through a second or third time. It is, however, of use to most people if you take notes on the arguments and ideas presented. Use the questions above to help you record what you think. Like all skills you need to practise and try out different methods and find the way that enables you to take in the information most easily. Whilst you are reading you will come across parts of the text that you think are important. You may want to write these out in full as you may use them as quotations in your own writing.

Remember to make a note of the author, date, book title, publisher, place of publication and the page you have taken the text from as you will need to include these in any academic assignment.

Journals

Educational journals provide up-to-date information about research on issues relating to education. There are journals published in relation to most curriculum subjects and for each educational sector. For those of you seeking a qualification many of these journals are available online and can be accessed using an Athens password. Your academic library will provide you with further information on journal access.

Libraries

You can buy many of the texts recommended in this book from good booksellers. Some of the texts are available from the government free of charge. You will, however, also need to use libraries to further your reading. Your local library will be able to order books for you but this may take a long time. It is a good idea to use your local college or university library to gain access to texts. If you have not used an academic library before it is advisable to book an induction session with a member of the library staff. They will be able to explain to you how the library is organised and how to find the text you want. They will also be able to provide you with information on accessing electronic texts, journals and online publications.

Keeping it all together!

Whilst you are studying you will be collecting materials. For example, a Foundation Degree usually takes up to three years of study and you will collect lots of information. You will collect your own notes from reading, notes from lectures, information from your workplace and your own collection of articles, and so forth. You will refer to these materials in your assignments and you need to think about where to keep them so that they are accessible.

Academic writing

Writing an assignment (essay) requires you to demonstrate some key skills. You may be asked to justify your reasons for doing something in a particular way. You may be asked to make recommendations for the future. You will need to be able to show what you know about a subject. This means being able to write about the key points or main arguments clearly. You will therefore need to show the reader that you have understood the points being made about a particular issue and provide some different points of view. You should also support what you write by referring to the texts you have read. You can do this by talking about what a particular author believes and you might even want to quote from them. Don't forget to present some arguments that differ from your own opinion but explain why you disagree with them using information from the authors you do believe are correct.

You should make connections between differing points of view and in some cases will need to link these to the practices you have observed in your workplace, providing reasons for your arguments. This means that you will have to 'reflect' on what you do. A reflective practitioner looks at their own actions identifying positive features and areas for development. Crucially, they try to understand why something happened in the way that it did.

When you are writing ask yourself the following questions:

➤ Am I using simple language to explain an idea?
➤ Do I understand what I have written?
➤ Can I support my argument by referring (linking) it to another writer, theory or idea?

It is very important to check what you have written. You may want to read it aloud to see if it sounds right. This will help you to spot any spelling errors, punctuation errors or typographical errors. If you have a sympathetic friend who will read it through for you, that is also a helpful check.

Referencing

An important part of academic writing is referencing. This demonstrates that you have read relevant texts and other materials. Referencing allows a reader to look at the same texts and materials that you have looked at if they so wish. When you reference you are acknowledging how the ideas contained in what you have read have helped you to complete your assignment. You should include a reference every time you directly quote a sentence or section of somebody else's work or when you write a summary of someone else's work. Within your writing, you will generally cite a reference using the author's surname and the date of the publication immediately following a summary of someone else's work. If you are making a direct quote from a source, you need to enable the reader to locate that quote immediately. The page number is therefore also included. If your writing is a summary of a number of different sources that said the same or similar things then you need to list these sources at the end of the sentence in chronological order. In some cases it is also helpful to insert the author reference citation into the text: e.g. 'As Barber (1996) indicates …'

At the end of any academic writing you need to provide a list of materials that you have used to help you. This is the reference list. The reference list contains all of the information that will enable the reader to find the material that you have used. You should only include in the reference list the sources that you have cited in the main text of the work. Therefore this should not be a list of everything you have read but only those that you referred to in your writing.

Bibliographies

A bibliography is attached to the end of an assignment. It lists all of the books, articles and other materials you have used when writing the assignment. It is not restricted to items referred to in the text. Each item in a bibliography contains information which is presented in the following order:

➤ Author's surname and initials (full stops after each initial).
➤ Year of publication.
➤ Title of article.
➤ Title of publication. i.e. book, periodical, etc. (underlined or italicised).

➤➤ Volume number or numbers of volumes, if applicable.
➤➤ Number of the edition, if other than the first.
➤➤ Editor, compiler or selector, if other than the author.
➤➤ Place of publication.
➤➤ Publisher.
➤➤ Page number or number, if applicable.

Referencing is a difficult skill. If you are studying at a college or university you will be able to get advice and guidance on referencing. Every academic organisation has a favoured system of referencing that they like you to follow. Make sure that you are given their guidelines and that you ask for clarification if this information is not clear.

Conclusion

In this chapter we have introduced you to some skills that will enable you to be successful in your studies. You will have identified your preferred learning style and begun to think about the practicalities of studying. We have also provided you with an overview of the contents of this book which will enable you to access information quickly.

 References

Barber, M. (1996) *The Learning Game: Arguments for an Educational Revolution*, London: Victor Gollancz.

Annotated Bibliography

Cottrell, S. (1999) *The Study Skills Handbook*, London: Macmillan. This book provides an introduction to learning styles and offers practical advice on how to study effectively.

Chapter 2

Personal and professional development and the role of the Teaching Assistant

This chapter sets out to discuss both the current role and professional development of the Teaching Assistant (TA). Over recent history we have seen a vast increase in the number of TAs in schools (Vincett *et al* 2005). This increase can be attributed to a number of factors including: the National Agreement which will be discussed further in the chapter; the implementation of statutory Planning, Preparation and Assessment (PPA) time for all teaching staff; budget changes in schools; the increase in academic qualifications within the sector and routes into teacher training, and the professionalisation of the workforce.

I'll name that support worker in one!

Most literature will refer to those working in education as teachers or support staff. Support staff is the generic title given to those who work to support learners. This includes secretaries, midday assistants, site managers, caretakers and those who work to support teaching and learning. Those people engaged in supporting teaching and learning have been variously referred to as Learning Support Assistants, Teaching Assistants, or Classroom Assistants with the term 'Teaching Assistant' or 'TA' currently being preferred (DfES 2000). Within the profession however, especially on the 'shop floor', the matter seems unresolved (Hancock and Colloby 2005). We use the term TA throughout this book to prevent confusion although in our experience job titles seem to be arbitrarily fixed within local contexts. In addition, TAs are employed in a variety of educational sectors. This confusion over the title of TAs is mirrored in a lack of clarity about the roles a TA is expected to do. Consider the effects of workforce remodelling. Is this making a difference to perceptions of the role of TA?

What do Teaching Assistants really do?

We know that to ask TAs what they do in their day-to-day routine would encompass a huge list of duties, from planning, assessment, managing, supporting, first aid duties and yes, some would be washing paint pots. Teaching Assistants are employed to undertake various tasks. Many find it difficult to obtain job descriptions from their employer and this is sometimes because everyone is a little unclear about what is and is not part of the role. What we do know is that the role is changing and evolving.

In 2000 the DfES produced the document *Working with Teaching Assistants: A Good Practice Guide* (DfES 2000). This document not only sets out to describe the role of the TA but also their management and deployment within organisations. As if to demonstrate how hard it is to sum up exactly what the TA's role includes, the document split the support that a TA provides into four sections.

➤➤ Support for the pupil.
➤➤ Support for the teacher.
➤➤ Support for the curriculum.
➤➤ Support for the school.

These four separate and yet overlapping themes are found throughout the literature about Teaching Assistants, the National Standards for Teaching Assistants and the Higher Level Teaching Assistant Standards (DfES 2003).

If you asked a TA what the greater part of their job involved most would talk about supporting learners. This includes work such as supporting Special Educational Needs (SEN) and statemented pupils in mainstream education; working one-to-one or in small groups; listening to readers; and helping disabled learners access the curriculum. As a result of this work TAs build up a valuable insight into a learner's attainment which can be invaluable to a teacher. After all, the TA may have worked one-to-one with a learner for several hours a day and therefore have built up a strong bond with them. Thus this criterion crosses over with that of support for the teacher. TAs may also support teachers by taking on some administrative tasks and some will be involved in assisting with the planning and assessment of lessons. Whilst this indicates that a TA may carry out many similar duties and tasks to that of a teacher, the learners may even refer to a TA as a teacher, it is the teacher that manages the learning and assessment taking place. At present a TA should not take on these management duties without direct guidance and assistance from a teacher.

When thinking about how TAs support the curriculum it becomes apparent that the duties described above may also provide curriculum support. Many TAs, especially those within the secondary school sector, are working within departments, rather than with specific year groups or individual learners. This allows the TA to become more familiar with the staff within the department, raise their own subject knowledge and enables them to become part of the departmental team. A head of department is then able to target the support of a TA where it is most needed. In some schools TAs have a department of their own with learners being sent to them at particular points during the week. Within the primary school sector some TAs support literacy or numeracy throughout the school, whilst others may support or teach music or another foundation subject.

All of the TA's work could also be described as providing support for the school; for example, when school achievement is raised; when TAs support and embody the school's ethos through their practices; through TAs working within the school team and community and even when they attend functions such as summer fairs, productions and plays. They may support their organisation through attending open evenings or working within a faculty team. Much of this work is an intrinsic part of the role whatever sector the TAs work in and the extra-curricular activities are done out of goodwill as these are not paid.

Specialist Teaching Assistants and Higher Level Teaching Assistants

There are two key groups of TA' to whom the label Specialist Teaching Assistant (STA) applies. The first of those are TAs who have gained an STA qualification, for example from the Open University. The others are TA's who are employed to work specifically in one area, for example classroom display. This discrepancy adds to a feeling of confused understandings about what the TA's role should encompass, Teaching Assistants themselves being possibly the least likely to be told. The qualifications for Specialist Teaching Assistants were launched in the late 1990s to train serving Teaching Assistants in primary schools in the knowledge and skills necessary for assisting qualified teachers and supporting learning in reading, writing, numeracy and related skills at Key Stage 1 Level of the National Curriculum (www.dfes. gov.uk 2005). However clarification of the contents and level of training courses has been problematic. The qualification and level was dependent on which training provider ran the STA course. The Open University Specialist Teaching Assistant Course (STAC) rated as a 60 credit point/HE level 1 (Certificate level) qualification (Employers' Organisation 2004). However, locally organised STA courses sometimes differed in approach and level.

In 2003 the DfES launched the Higher Level Teaching Assistant (HLTA) standards (DfES 2003). The role of the HLTA was included in the National Agreement proposals (DfES 2003), which we will discuss later in this chapter. Again the HLTA post and HLTA standards are two different things. For a TA to become an HLTA they must either complete a training programme or if they are deemed to be near to meeting the standards they can follow an assessment route. Entry to HLTA training is dependent upon an application process. Once the assessor has agreed that the TA meets the standards then it is incumbent upon the TA either to take a job designated as HLTA or to negotiate the position within their own organisation. HLTA status does not necessarily lead to promotion or a rise in salary. The role of the HLTA will differ amongst schools. Many will carry on their original duties, others may gain more managerial duties such as Assistant Special Needs Coordinator (Assistant SENCO) (Wallace 2005). Certainly, 'hints and tips' for the role can be seen in the 25 Tasks, the set of duties derived from the National Agreement.

The National Agreement

> In January 2003, local employers, school workforce unions and the Department for Education and Skills signed a National Agreement that paved the way for radical reform of the school workforce to raise standards and tackle workload.
>
> (DfES 2003: 3)

The National Agreement has been the source of heated discussions in many staffrooms. Its full title – *Raising Standards and Tackling Workload: A National Agreement* includes the strategy, amongst others, to directly use TAs to reduce the workload of teachers in schools. This caused worry amongst the teaching profession that unqualified TAs would be used to replace teachers. The majority of the main teaching unions and other relevant bodies are still affiliated to the National Agreement, supporting its goals and strategies to reduce teachers' workloads. However, it is still the focus of much debate and the National Union of Teachers (NUT), the largest teachers' union, has disagreed with some of the strategies, such as the use of TA's to cover classes; claiming that the 'proposals would undermine the quality of education being offered to pupils. It seems like a cheap way of addressing teacher shortages.' (Hinds 2002). Despite the absence of the NUT the agreement was still signed and agreed by the remaining unions and bodies.

Planning, preparation and assessment

> From 1 September 2005, all teachers are entitled to a minimum 10 percent of their timetable teaching time guaranteed for planning, preparation and assessment (PPA).
>
> (http://www.remodelling.org/ppa_support.php 2005)

The implementation of PPA time has had an impact upon the management of teacher timetables. All teaching staff have an allocation of time away from the classroom to carry out planning, preparation and assessment. Some schools have chosen to deploy TAs as cover for teachers. Nevertheless, headteachers have the worry of trying to organise classroom cover within limited budgets and are having to make creative use of TAs or other staff. The difficulty of reconciling the need for highly trained staff to ensure continuity of teaching and learning for all pupils with budget difficulties was one reason why the National Association of Head Teachers (NAHT) chose to withdraw from the National Agreement in March 2005 (Curtis 2005), only to be threatened and forced to comply with the agreement by the government.

The long-term consequence for TAs of these developments are yet to be seen. We are currently witnessing a rise in the number of higher level qualifications for TAs, including HLTA and Foundation Degrees. Whether these Foundation Degree graduates extend their studies to full degrees and therefore create a new post-graduate TA role is to be seen. However if headteachers are struggling to pay existing teachers and NQTs, will they be able to offer a competitive salary for graduate TAs?

The 25 Tasks

The 25 Tasks, often known as the 24 Tasks (number 14 was not implemented until September 2005), were part of the National Agreement and implemented in 2003 to lower teachers' workloads. The agreement does not force TAs to carry out these duties; however, it can be seen how many of the tasks fall easily into the remit of the TA. Figure 2.1 below is taken from the National Remodelling Team website and shows how the Tasks have been incorporated into School Teachers' Pay and Conditions.

Remodelling

> At the heart of the national remodelling programme is a fundamental belief that deep-seated change can and does occur. What it requires are new attitudes and behaviours, new beliefs and values, and new skills and capabilities to be created and, importantly, sustained.
>
> (http://www.remodelling.org/what_is.php 2005)

Figure 2.1 The 25 Tasks

National Agreement list	Annex 5, School Teachers' Pay and Conditions (STPCD) – Tasks no longer required to be undertaken by Teachers
1	Collecting money;	Collecting money from pupils and parents.
2	Chasing absences – teachers will need to inform the relevant member of staff when students are absent from their class or from school;	Investigating a pupil's absence.
3	Bulk photocopying;	Bulk photocopying.
4	Copy typing;	Typing or making word-processed versions of manuscript material and producing revisions of such versions.
5	Producing standard letters – teachers may be required to contribute as appropriate in formulating the content of standard letters;	Word-processing, copying and distributing bulk communications, including standard letters, to parents and pupils.
6	Producing class lists – teachers may be required to be involved as appropriate in allocating students to a particular class;	Producing class lists on the basis of information provided by teachers.
7	Record keeping and filing – teachers may be required to contribute to the content of records;	Keeping and filing records, including records based on data supplied by teachers.
8	Classroom display – teachers will make professional decisions in determining what material is displayed in and around their classroom;	Preparing, setting up and taking down classroom displays in accordance with decisions taken by teachers.
9	Analysing attendance figures – it is for teachers to make use of the outcome of analysis;	Producing analyses of attendance figures.
10	Processing exam results – teachers will need to use the analysis of exam results;	Producing analyses of examination results.
11	Collating pupil reports;	Collating pupil reports.
12	Administering work experience – teachers may be required to support pupils on work experience (including through advice and visits);	Administration of work experience (but not selecting placements and supporting pupils by advice or visits).
13	Administering examinations – teachers have a professional responsibility for identifying appropriate examinations for their pupils;	Administration of public and internal examinations.
14	Invigilating examinations – see distinct provisions below;	[Not required before September 2005.]
15	Administering teacher cover;	Administration of cover for absent teachers.
16	ICT trouble shooting and minor repairs;	Ordering, setting up and maintaining ICT equipment and software.

continued…

Figure 2.1 continued

17	Commissioning new ICT equipment;	[See 16.]
18	Ordering supplies and equipment – teachers may be involved in identifying needs;	Ordering supplies and equipment.
19	Stocktaking;	[See 20.]
20	Cataloguing, preparing, issuing and maintaining equipment and materials;	Cataloguing, preparing, issuing and maintaining materials and equipment and stocktaking the same.
21	Minuting meetings – teachers may be required to communicate action points from meetings;	Taking verbatim notes or producing formal minutes of meetings.
22	Co-ordinating and submitting bids – teachers may be required to make a professional input into the content of bids;	Coordinating and submitting bids (for funding, school status and the like) using contributions by teachers and others.
23	Seeking and giving personnel advice;	[Covered in paragraph 62.11, not in Annex 5.]
24	Managing pupil data – teachers will need to make use of the analysis of pupil data;	Managing the data in school management systems.
25	Inputting pupil data – teachers will need to make the initial entry of pupil data into school management systems.	Transferring manual data about pupils not covered by the above into computerised school management systems.

Remodelling is a process to be undertaken by all schools to reduce workloads and work as effectively as possible, and in fact constitutes multiple initiatives being run at once. The National Remodelling Team (2005a) describe workforce remodelling as:

➤➤ a self-directed approach that places the school in control of its own change agenda

➤➤ recognising that schools must formulate unique solutions to common problems – one size doesn't fit all

➤➤ relying on the involvement and participation of the entire school community

➤➤ revolving around a change process that is a tried-and-tested way of managing change in schools

➤➤ underpinned by a wide network of support involving LEAs, the NRT and the signatory organisations

Schools are asked to steer through the process using a School Change Team (SCT). This process of change will alter the role of TAs in different ways; for example, one school may wish to enhance their ICT provision and plan to train a TA to manage an ICT drop-in centre for pupils and staff.

 **Task 2A**

What remodelling processes have happened in your school?
How are they going to impact upon your role?

Management of Teaching Assistants

The management of TAs within schools is a major indicator of how effective the school can be (DfES 2000). The simplest example of this would be the deployment and training of TAs. Key questions might include: Where are TAs placed and for how long? What access to professional development do they have?

In response to the increase in support staff in the late 1990s, and in anticipation of the National Agreement, HLTA and qualifications such as Foundation Degrees developed. The DfES published *Working with Teaching Assistants: A Good Practice Guide* (2000). The booklet was designed to assist those managing TAs and gives good practice examples on a range of aspects of TA management from creating partnerships with teachers to reviewing performance and promoting development. A summary of suggestions can be seen in Figure 2.2.

 Task 2B

How many of these good practice suggestions are carried out within your establishment?

From those not currently employed within the organisation, how many could be included, relatively easily?

Think back to your own induction and current practice. How much of a difference would it make to your role if all of these suggestions were to be enforced in your organisation?

Individual case studies can be found at the Teachernet website (www.teachernet.gov.uk) which demonstrates how schools have successfully included, developed, deployed and/or managed TAs within the organisation.

The future of the Teaching Assistant

The numbers of TAs deployed within education has risen rapidly over the past five years and it is not yet clear when this increase will end. The profile of the TA is also changing and diversifying alongside different roles being created for them within educational organisations. Far from the profession declining we seem to be entering a period of sustained growth and opportunity. We will now consider some of the newly created roles for TAs in greater depth.

Learning mentors

Learning mentors work with learners on an individual basis. The work that they carry out may not only be to support learning but can also, and often does, take on a pastoral role. Learning mentors have a responsibility for concentrating on a learner's attendance, lateness, behaviour, bullying, social cohesion and emotional development. Learning mentors may be employed across sectors and much of the role lies outside of the classroom (Hancock and Colloby 2005). The authors note that they know of schools within their own geographical area, where the role of 'Learning Mentor' has been enthusiastically taken up by men. There is however, a lack of research to indicate whether or not this practice is more widely spread.

Figure 2.2 Working with Teaching Assistants

Defining responsibilities	*Deployment*	*Partnerships with teachers*	*Partnerships with others in education*	*Partnership among Teaching Assistants*	*Reviewing performance and promoting development*
Knowing school policy	Clear line management	Clarifying both roles	Working with outside agencies	Regular TA meetings	Regular appraisal
Suitable appointments	Appropriate line manager	TA plans with teacher	Meetings with SENCO	Sharing information about pupils	Reviewing job description
Suitable contracts	Deployment location	Climate to encourage high-quality TA input	Communications with parents	Sharing information about the school	Assessing TA training needs
Job description	Continuity of work	Feedback mechanisms	Communications with ethnic minority communities	Information about support groups	Providing induction
Induction	Teamwork	Teacher guidance on behaviour management	Inviting TAs to participate in school functions	Liaison with staff governors	Use of mentors
Communication	Giving the TA the wider picture	TA informed of developments with SEN children			Examining different forms of training
	Giving the TA specific information	TAs included at IEP reviews			Undertaking joint training
	Confidentiality	TAs invited to staff meetings			Share what is learned
	Reviewing the TA–pupil Link	TAs included in the staffroom			Professional development portfolio
	Using Special Skills	TAs included in written comments			Finding finance
		Legal responsibilities of the TA			Evaluate training
		Review classroom relationships			

It is nevertheless interesting to contemplate this issue for instance why might men be attracted to this role especially given that the TA profession is predominantly female?

Display assistants

Display assistants manage the displays and other visual messages around the organisation. They ensure that displays are educational, interactive and meaningful to the learners working in partnership with and under the direction of a teacher. Display Assistants will also carry out duties such as mounting work. This role seems to have developed directly as a result of one of the 24 Tasks, in which teachers do not have to put up displays. There is none the less some resistance from teachers who feel that this is an integral part of their own role, the classroom display providing a great learning opportunity but also adding to the ethos of the classroom and organisation.

Assistant SENCO

As discussed earlier, the Assistant Special Educational Needs Coordinator (SENCO) will support the work of the SENCO, especially in larger schools. The Assistant SENCO may assist by reviewing Individual Education Plans, take a line-management responsibility for other TAs and prepare material for annual statutory reviews (Wallace 2005).

School links mentors

This title varies widely between organisations but involves moving and working with students of secondary school age in Further Education colleges and other places of vocational training. Although the FE teacher remains in charge of the learning and assessment, the TA will be the responsible adult from the school and as such play a significant role in the management of the student's learning, assessment and most importantly behaviour.

Cover Supervisors

The role of a Cover Supervisor is to provide cover for lessons. These may be planned teacher absences such as those linked to PPA time or staff development, or may be unplanned such as providing cover for staff illness. The Cover Supervisor may be a qualified teacher or a TA. The role can be viewed as a hybrid of Teacher and TA as Cover Supervisors do not manage the curriculum which remains the responsibility of a qualified teacher, but payment for this post is greater than that of a TA. This is a role that is developing within schools though there is some resistance to it as it can be seen as a direct challenge to the teaching profession. It is also unclear about whether cover supervisors should hold a qualification to perform the role.

Continual Professional Development of the TA

We have already looked at examples of Continual Professional Development (CPD) for the TA. This section aims to provide you with a further explanation of the available qualifications. It must be noted that qualifications are continually changing and developing and it is always best to consult College/University tutors and/or Careers Advisors for the latest information.

Levels

When beginning to consider professional training many TAs face a confusing array of information. One of the first things that TA's need to understand, is the relevant levels of the programmes on offer. Figure 2.3 shows how levels within vocational courses, such as National Vocational Qualifications (NVQs) can be compared to more academic course such as GCSEs by using the National Qualifications Framework (NQF).

Entry level qualifications – NVQ Teaching Assistants

Currently the NVQ Teaching Assistants Levels 2 and 3 are the most requested qualification for many TAs. This course allows TAs to gain confidence in their work in schools and gain a good basic level of understanding of what goes on in the workplace. Colleges and LEAs will differ in entry criteria, length of course and cost. This qualification is not age specific. In addition to NVQ programmes there are many more relevant courses available, including qualifications in Child Care and in Early Years. The list is quite extensive.

HLTA

The Higher Level Teaching Assistant status has already been discussed in this chapter. TAs wishing to enter a programme will need to contact their local awarding body such as the LEA. More information can also be obtained at www.hlta.gov.uk. It must be stressed that HLTA, via the 50-day training route or on the assessment route, will allow the candidate to claim the HLTA status associated with a specific vacancy in a school. It is not a qualification similiar to the NVQ that can be used 'universally'.

Foundation degrees

Foundation degrees can be obtained in many subjects. They are distinguished from a 'standard' degree taken at a university in several ways. First, they have to be vocationally based, for example you can do a Foundation Degree for Teaching Assistants because it is a vocational course and therefore you need to be a TA to do it. Second, they are equivalent to the first two-thirds of a 'standard' degree. For example, a standard degree is typically three years long. The Foundation Degree is equivalent to the first two years of the degree. Foundation Degrees for Teaching Assistants are aimed at TAs and provide them with both a good understanding of and knowledge about the TA's role together with developing their academic ability. Foundation Degrees can lead to the candidate moving on to complete a full Bachelor's Degree. Some Universities offer a Level Three course to convert the Foundation Degree into a full Bachelor's Degree. Holders of a Bachelor's Degree may be eligible to apply for teacher training programmes such as the Post-Graduate Certificate in Education (PGCE) or the Graduate Teacher Training Programme (GTTP) for primary teaching although would they need to build up a greater subject specialism for teaching programmes in other sectors.

Figure 2.3 The National Qualification Framework

Framework for higher educational qualifications		National Qualification Framework	
D	(Doctoral) Doctorates	8	Vocational diplomas
M	(Master's) Master's degrees, postgraduate certificates and diplomas	7	Key skills Vocational certificates and diplomas [NVQ 5]
H	(Honours) Bachelor's degrees with honours, graduate certificates and diplomas	6	Vocational certificates and diplomas
I	(Intermediate) Foundation degrees, ordinary (Bachelor's) degrees, Diplomas of Higher Education and Further Education, Higher National Diplomas	5	Key skills Vocational certificates and diplomas [NVQ 4]
C	(Certificate) Certificates of Higher Education	4	Vocational certificates and diplomas
		3	Key skills Vocational certificates and diplomas A levels [NVQ3]
		2	Key skills Vocational certificates and diplomas GCSE (Grades A*–C) [NVQ2]
		1	Key skills Vocational certificates and diplomas GCSE (Grades D*–G) [NVQ1]
		Entry level	Basic skills Entry level certificates

GTTP

The Graduate Teacher Training Programme (GTTP) enables graduates to train to be teachers within schools. It is a more hands on training approach when compared to a PGCE. Candidates need a relevant degree and apply to awarding bodies, usually an LEA or a university.

Conclusion

This chapter has introduced you to some of the changes in the employment of Teaching Assistants over the last decade. We have also considered the complex and differing roles that may be required of a TA. As a profession the role of Teachng Assistant is still in its infancy and we are likely to see many exciting developments over the coming years and in particular those arising from structural changes to the school workforce. We have also looked at some basic study skills and contemplated a few of the myriad of professional development courses available to you. Don't forget that if you wish to read further then use the bibliography section for this chapter.

📖 Bibliography

Curtis, P. (2005) 'Headteachers pull out of workforce agreement', *Guardian Education* (17 March 2005).

DfES (2000) *Working with Teaching Assistants: A Good Practice Guide*, London: DfES.

DfES (2003) *Professional Standards for Higher Level Teaching Assistants*, London: DfES.

Employers' Organisation for Local Government (2004) *Qualifications for Teaching Assistants Version 2*, www.lg-employers.gov.uk, London: Employers' Organisation for Local Government.

Hancock, R. and Colloby, J. (2005) 'Eight titles and roles', in Hancock, R. and Collins, J. (eds) *Primary Teaching Assistants Learners and Learning*, London: David Fulton Publishers.

Hinds, D. (2002) 'Fresh roles and a choice of fulfilment', *Times Educational Supplement* (6 December 2002).

National Remodelling Team (2003) 'Raising standards and tackling workload – a national agreement', http://www.remodelling.org/downloads/9.pdf#search='national%20agreement'

National Remodelling Team (2005a) 'About remodelling', http://www.remodelling.org/what_is.php

National Remodelling Team (2005b) 'Are there different versions of the 24 tasks?', http://www.remodelling.org/diff_ver_24t.php

National Remodelling Team (2005c) 'PPA support', http://www.remodelling.org/ppa_support.php

Press Association (2005) 'Kelly orders heads to implement workforce reform', *Guardian Education* (23 March 2005).

Sage, R. and Wilkie, M. (2004) *Supporting Learning in Primary Schools*, 2nd edn, Exeter: Learning Matters.

Vincett, K., Cremin, H. and Thomas, G. (2005) *Teachers and Assistants Working Together*, Buckingham: Open University Press.

Wallace, S. (2005) 'Being a SENCO Assistant', in Hancock, R. and Collins, J. (eds) *Primary Teaching Assistants: Learners and Learning*, London: David Fulton Publishers.

Circular number 13/97

http://www.dfes.gov.uk/publications/guidanceonthelaw/13_97/partb_20.htm

The National Agreement

http://www.hlta.gov.uk
http://www.teachernet.gov.uk
http://www.remodelling.org/downloads/9.pdf#search='national%20agreement')

Workforce remodelling

http://www.remodelling.org/what_is.php 2005)

Chapter 3

Growth, development and learning

This chapter will introduce theories about parenting styles and the impact these have upon learning. Child development is explained through the use of psychoanalytical, cognitive and learning theories. We go on to look at motivation which is of key importance for learning and linked to this the physiological, cognitive and humanist theories of motivation along with the concept of emotional intelligence.

Child rearing: practices and styles

The way that we care for children is influenced by our own experiences of being a child. 'Parenting' is not a term exclusive to being the genetic parent and can refer to a number of types of carer such as guardians and foster parents. Our memories of the parenting we received from those who cared for us will have helped us develop a blueprint of how to care for a child. Consider the following experience of 'Hannah'. (Extract 1)

Extract 1: Hannah

Hannah lived with her mother and brother. Her parents had been unhappy together and had separated when Hannah was five. Hannah's mother now found it difficult to make ends meet and so took a job that involved long hours. As a result Hannah and her brother had to go to their Gran's house before and after school as her mother left the house early and returned late. Hannah's mother was always tired and bad tempered. When they all arrived home at night there were jobs to be done and Hannah's mother had her hands full trying to keep on top of it all. Although Hannah and her brother did do jobs around the house, they still managed to create a mess when they played. Hannah's mother found this very difficult to cope with and regularly smacked the children and shouted at them for causing this mess. She also had no patience with the children if they spilled or dropped anything. Sometimes Hannah's mother threw things at them.

As a grown adult with children Hannah often finds that she over reacts to her children making a mess. Whilst she doesn't throw things at them she does shout and yell. She realises that she is just repeating patterns of behaviour set by her mother but can't always stop herself. She feels very guilty afterwards and tries to make it up to the children by taking them out for a treat. Hannah is worried that her children will be influenced by her behaviour in the same way that she was influenced by her mother.

Whether or not Hannah's memories were strictly accurate, it is now generally agreed that perceptions about childhood experiences affect the way we deal with our own children. There are a whole variety of theories about what might be important in family life, current research particularly emphasising the importance of children being offered warmth and affection, structure and rules and where carers take time to listen. Parenting styles can be categorised using four different basic approaches.

Approach One: Authoritarian – identified by Baumrind (1973). As Glasgow *et al.* (1997) point out, authoritarian carers try to shape their children through controlling their behaviour and their attitudes. They also encourage their children to have respect for authority and object to children arguing with them.

Approach Two: Permissive – identified by Baumrind (1973). This is an approach to parenting that allows children to be in control. As children's opinions are indulged and valued this can mean the child becomes demanding and sometimes aggressive, particularly where such behaviour is not challenged by the carers. According to Maccoby and Martin (1983) they are also likely to be less independent and may do less well at school.

Approach Three: Authoritative – identified by Baumrind (1973). This approach to parenting combines the best characteristics of the two former styles. Carers are warm and caring and surround the child with clear structures and demands whilst still listening to the child's needs. This is seen as the most favourable of the approaches. Boyes and Allen (1993) believe that this approach leads to children being capable of higher levels of moral reasoning.

Approach Four: Neglecting – identified by Maccoby and Martin (1983). Children in this model are insecure and have problems forming relationships. They tend to be antisocial, less involved in their schooling and act on impulse. Pittman and Chase-Lansdale (2001) argue that these children become sexually active at an earlier age.

Cultural differences in the values attached to particular social processes, such as education, mean that the approaches identified above do not necessarily apply to all ethnic groups. Thus different cultural groups have different customs, traditions, values, views and beliefs. For example, in the Asian culture caring and warmth are valued, as is being very strict. Child rearing also differs from the perspective of how families are structured and the period of time in which children were reared. For instance we can return to the example of Hannah who was brought up in a single-parent household thirty years ago. The attitudes of people to single parent households would have been rather different than they are now. Prejudice against single parents may have made the situation stressful for both Hannah and her mother. If Hannah's Gran hadn't 'helped out' perhaps her mother wouldn't have been able to work. So in order to understand the child-rearing context there are a number of complex and interrelated influences that need to be taken into account.

One of the most influential attachments in a child's life has long been thought to be that with his or her mother. However recent evidence has called this assumption into question.

Authors, such as Carr *et al.* (1991) argue that this notion is based on a small sample of societies where the mother has been the primary carer. In reality, children have a wide network of relationships that can include their wider family members, friends, neighbours and perhaps other carers such as nursery nurses. In addition, children can have a 'stable' well-adjusted life whether brought up by parents or by another carer (McGuire and Richman 1986). In other words children who attend day care because their mothers return to work after maternity leave have been shown to be just as stable as any other child although as Melhuish *et al.* (1990a) argue, there is some evidence to suggest that they may be less timid and more sociable.

Task 3A

Consider your own experiences as a parent or as a child receiving parenting. Which of Baumrind's parenting styles have you experienced?

Write a 150 word overview of your experiences that considers models of parenting styles.

It can be difficult to reflect upon your parenting experiences. You should not be concerned if you discover that you are a permissive parent as opposed to an authoritative parent. The key point to remember is that parenting styles may affect learning but they are one of a range of factors that we need to consider with regard to child development and learning.

Child development: three theories

There are three major theories that have had an impact on the way in which we look at children's development, how they relate to adults and how they relate to their environment. These are the psychoanalytical, cognitive and learning theories.

Psychoanalytical theory

The first of these theories to be considered is psychoanalytical theory. This theory is most often associated with Sigmund Freud (1856–1939). Freud developed his ideas about the way people behave on the basis of his own observations of children, adults and animals. He developed the idea that the human libido (sex drive) formed the root of a lot of their actions and interactions. Freud believed that it is the libido that enables us to care for one another even when there are no apparent sexual intentions in the relationship. For Freud the personality consists of three parts:

➤➤ The **id** is about fulfilling instinctive needs, such as a newborn baby suckling as milk enables it to survive.
➤➤ The **ego** develops later in a child's life and allows him or her to rationalise and plan in order to satisfy his or her instinctive needs. This involves learning, thinking, evaluating and perceiving.

➤→   Finally, the **superego** is about developing a conscience and understanding of what people should be like as an ideal. This aspect of the personality is formed through childhood experiences and the teachings of carers.

There are many who now argue with Freud's ideas. His research was certainly limited to a small sample of people and has been shown to be unscientific. In addition, his views on women have attracted much criticism from feminists as they are based on the idea of male superiority. Nevertheless, Freud's theories have had a tremendous influence on understanding human development and have only recently been challenged.

Cognitive theory

The second theory is cognitive theory. Cognitive theories are concerned with the study of understanding the act of knowing, perceiving or conceiving something '*as an act or faculty distinct from emotion and volition*' (*The Oxford Dictionary of Current English*, 1985), rather than with the development of the personality. We will begin by introducing Piaget's four stage theory.

Jean Piaget (1896–1980) believed that children were actively involved in structuring their own cognitive development through exploration of their environment. Children need to have real experiences and objects to discover things for themselves. The adult's role is to provide the experiences and objects for the child in order to facilitate the child's instinctive ability to think and learn. Children only learn when they are ready for different experiences as determined by their stage of cognitive development. Piaget believed that children interact with the environment and relate new knowledge to existing knowledge in a three-stage process of interaction. This consists of:

➤→   *Assimilation*: the need for further information
➤→   *Accommodation*: the need for organised information;
➤→   *Adaptation*: the need for revised and up to date information

Piaget described internal mental processes as *schemas* and the ways in which they are used during thinking as *operations*. These continually develop as we get new information about the world.

> In our society, children learn to do typical things during successive age periods. These things are very physical and concrete in infancy, becoming quite abstract in young adulthood. There is a period in between, from 6 years of age to 16, which in most Western countries spans the years of compulsory schooling. That is no accident; it is when the children learn how to handle symbol systems.
>
> (Biggs and Moore, 1993:60)

Piaget's research led him to believe that there were four major stages, each growing out of the one preceding it and each consisting of a complete organisation of concepts, strategies and assumptions. (Bee 2000). See Figure 3.1.

Figure 3.1 Piaget's stages of development

Stage	Age (approx)	Nature of schemas	Typical adaptations
Sensory-motor	Birth to 2 years	Practical action	Can act intentionally on the world, object permanence
Pre-operational	2 to 6 or 7 years	Symbolic (but not logical)	Can symbolise, talk about past and future, judgements showing egocentrism and moral realism
Concrete operational	6 or 7 to about		
11 years	Logical and mathematical	Can deal with two or more aspects of a situation at the same time, can decentre and conserve	
Formal operations	11 years (or so) onwards	Logical and mathematical abstractions	Formalism of physics and higher maths, morality based on intentions

Piaget thought that virtually all infants began with the same skills and built-in strategies and that their understanding and theories about how the world worked came from their active exploration of the environment. He did not think that the environment shaped the child, but rather the child actively seeks to understand its environment. Piaget concluded, from his experiences with IQ testing, that children's minds were organised differently to those of adults. He began to think that what distinguished children's thought from that of adults was not the sheer amount of knowledge, but the complexity and type of thought. It was this that inspired him to research the mental structures (schemas) of children as they grow.

Initially, in the sensory-motor stage, the infant will make sense of the world through their reflexes, sensory perceptions and physical actions upon objects and the world. They will learn to bang objects, suck them, turn and drop them. This allows them to develop a 'practical' or 'sensorimotor' knowledge of objects in time and space. Towards the end of this stage they can appreciate that an object will continue to exist even though it is out of sight.

The pre-operational stage consists of mental operations whereby the child realises that actions can be performed upon objects, but that they don't have to take place in reality. They can be performed 'in the head', perhaps using imagery. This stage is also the time when an understanding of symbols and what they represent in reallife develops. Hence the development of language symbol systems and drawing.

The concrete-operational stage is characterised by the ability to reason about the world of objects, time, number, space, causality, and is not confined to acting physically on the world. Children begin to grasp that the number of objects remain the same despite being rearranged, or that the mass of an object will remain the same even though its shape has been altered, or that a scene will contain the same elements despite being viewed from a different angle.

The formal-operational stage comes into being during adolescence. The adolescent is able to think in a logical fashion, is able to hypothesise, test and revise in the light of the results. This may occur practically or mentally, but it is an indication that the adolescent has achieved the end state of human cognition.

There are many aspects of Piaget's research which have been recognised as being valid, but questions are asked about others. For example, he is accused of a lack of attention to children's emotions in his pursuit of understanding logic. His detailed observations did indicate an appreciation of the interaction between thought and feelings but he was more concerned with identifying at what level of intellect a child may think, rather than what kinds of things he thought about. Margaret Donaldson (1986), a critic of Piaget, believed that there were many problems associated with the way in which tasks were presented to children. She argued that the context of the tasks makes a difference to understanding and that children are quite capable of logical thought earlier than Piaget suggested. Her arguments are centred on the fact that most reasoning is embedded both in a particular context and in the knowledge we already have. (Lee and Gupta 1995)

Piaget's stages of development are based on children failing certain tasks at certain ages which led him to believe that they do not possess the required mental structure at that stage. Others, like Donaldson, have shown that, in certain cases, they fail because they are not aware that they should use skills they already possess. This would indicate that the clear-cut stages of development are rather more blurred. Piaget's stair-like sequence, one stage growing out of the preceding stage, is likely to blend one stage into another with much overlap. In *The Learning Revolution* Dryden and Vos claim that, whilst there are

> definite stages of brain growth, physical growth and in the development of sensory learning ... Piaget's worst legacy is in the education systems using his theories to justify not exposing young children to experiences when their senses are ideally developed to benefit.
>
> (Dryden and Vos 2001: 111)

Vygotsky's (1896–1934) theory was centred on understanding the origins of the learner's knowledge. He agreed with Piaget on 'activity' being the basis for learning and the development of thinking, but there was a greater emphasis on the role of communication, social interaction and instruction in determining the path of development. He concluded that the more complex forms of thinking had their origins in the social interactions of children and adults and not merely in the learner's private explorations and understanding. He believed that the interactions with adults and peers, as well as instruction, were essential to cognitive development. His theory allowed for the impact of cultural context on development. He gave equal importance to intrinsic (individual) and external (cultural) forces, but in practice he focussed on the impact of culture on the young learner. The instruction of adults or peers is essential to reach the highest levels of thinking possible during each 'stage' (Lee and Gupta 1995). Vygotsky believed it was educationally more informative to know what the learner could do with some slight assistance than to know what could be achieved independently. This led to his concept of the 'zone of proximal development'. The 'zone of proximal development' is the gap between what a learner can do individually and what can be achieved with the help of a skilled or knowledgeable other. It is a range of tasks too hard for a learner to do on their own, but tasks they can manage with guidance. As they become more skilled the 'zone' shifts to include harder tasks. *'The key being in the language the adult uses to describe or frame the task'* (Bee 2000: 20). Later they use the same language to work independently. Therefore their learning is guided by an adult who 'models' and structures the learning experience.

Jerome Bruner (1915–), influenced by Vygotsky, believed that the social and cultural experiences played a major role in mental development. He called the 'modelling' and 'structuring' of the learning environment 'scaffolding' and believed that to learn a given skill, one had to be equipped with other prerequisite skills. He concluded that learning involved the search for pattern, regularity and predictability and instruction served to assist the learner in the formation and discovery of such patterns and rules. This is known as *'social constructivism'*. Bruner, like Piaget, recognised the biological and evolutionary constraints on human intelligence, but differed on the actual construction of that development. Piaget's theory was based on the active constructive nature of human development and was known as the *'constructivist'* approach.

Learning theories

Although 'learning' is often associated with educational environments such as schools or colleges, most learning takes place outside of such environments. Learning occurs when there is a 'spontaneous' desire to master something for oneself; to understand those sounds and meanings which others around you are using, to struggle to stand up and walk around like all the others you watch, the 'mastery' of such things is what prompts us to learn something. Equally there are many things that we do not learn spontaneously – such as labouring in the workshop, maths or moral codes of behaviour. It is believed by the learning theorists that rewards and punishments are the prompts for hard work and diligence as opposed to spontaneous self-mastery. There are two variations of a learning theory, classical conditioning and operant conditioning.

Classical conditioning

The essence of this type of learning is the association made between two events. First we must consider the response made by a baby when an 'unconditional' stimulus is given, such as a touch of the cheek. The baby will turn and try to suck. The learning occurs when a new stimulus or 'conditional' stimulus is put into the loop. So, for example, the mother sings a particular song and touches the baby's cheek, the baby turns to suck. If the mother just sings the particular song the baby will not turn to suck, but when the touch is combined with the song then she will. Eventually the baby will learn that the 'conditional' stimulus, the song, is also a cue to suck (Bee 2000). This theory was developed by a Russian physiologist called Ivan Pavlov (1849–1936). He discovered 'learning by association' and although his research was exclusively done with dogs, his findings are relevant to child development. He noticed that the dogs would salivate when the trainer entered with bowls of food. This is the 'unconditional' response any dog would give when faced with a bowl of food. Pavlov set about introducing a 'conditional' stimulus into the equation; the sound of a bell. The bell on its own, initially, would not incur the response of salivating. Gradually the dogs began to associate the bell with the food so at last the bell alone would bring about salivation. This can be put into human terms.

A child may learn to associate the nurse with a painful jab and burst into tears when he or she walks into the room. In this case, the jab is the unconditioned stimulus and the nurse is the conditioned one. Something which did not originally call forth the 'natural' response begins to do so by being associated with it.

(Sylva and Lunt 1982: 123)

Operant conditioning

This learning theory is characterised by a belief in the application of appropriate reinforcements to achieve the learning of a new response to an old behaviour. 'Reinforcement' is defined by its effect and the increased probability of reproducing the desired behaviour.

> *Positive reinforcement* – increases the chances that the behaviour will occur again e.g. when parents show pleasure and give praise when a child sits and listens quietly then the child is more likely to learn to sit and listen quietly.
> *Negative reinforcement* – occurs when something someone does which is unpleasant is stopped e.g. when a child that is ignored whinges but as soon as it is picked up the child stops whinging. This reinforces the child's notion that whinging will get results.

Both positive and negative reinforcements strengthen behaviour. In contrast, 'punishment' is intended to weaken undesired behaviour (Bee 2000).

Social cognitive theory

Bandura's (1989) theory supports the other traditional learning theories, but adds several key ideas:

> Learning from watching others – observational learning and modelling.
> Intrinsic reinforcement or rewards – those internal to the individual, such as pride or discovery.

Modelling can be a vehicle for learning abstract as well as concrete skills or information. In this abstract modelling, the observer extracts a rule that may be the basis of the model's behaviour, and then learns the rule as well as the specific behaviour. A child who sees his parents volunteering one day a month at a food bank may extract a rule about the importance of 'helping others', even if the parents never articulate this rule specifically. In this way a child or adult can acquire attitudes, values, ways of solving problems, even standards of self-evaluation through modelling.

(Bee 2000: 22)

Task 3B

Consider the similarities and differences between the psychoanalytical, cognitive development and learning theories. Summarise these in 250 words.

Figure 3.2 The learning cycle

1.	Prestructural – The task is engaged, but the learner is distracted or misled by an irrelevant aspect belonging to a previous stage (out to lunch!)
2.	Unistructural – The learner focuses on the relevant domain and picks up one aspect to work with (a one-eyed view of things!).
3.	Multistructural – The learner picks up more and more correct or relevant features, but does not integrate them together (all bricks, no house!).
4.	Relational – The learner now integrates the parts with each other, so that the whole has a coherent structure and meaning (home and housed!).
5.	Extended Abstract – The learner now generalises the structure to take in new and more abstract features, representing a higher level of thinking (pastures new!).

We all go through a 'learning cycle' at whatever 'stage' of development we are at. Whether we are looking at a baby, a six year old or an adult, the cycle remains the same, but the 'prerequisite' skills which we have will determine how long we spend at each 'level' in the cycle. Biggs and Moore (1993) conceptualise the learning cycle as a five-stage process. See Figure 3.2.

Child development – theories of motivation

As a Teaching Assistant, being able to identify what motivates learners to engage with learning is a powerful tool. Understanding motivation enables educators to structure teaching programmes to meet an individual learner's needs and can be of help in managing behaviour (see chapter 8). There are three key theories of motivation to consider:

1   *Physiological* – arousal and motivation
2   *Cognitive* – visualisation and motivational traits
3   *Humanist* – Maslow's Hierarchy of Needs

Physiological

This approach focuses mainly on the basic needs for survival which we have from birth.

> If we are hungry or thirsty, then we are motivated to reduce these needs by seeking out food and drink. Whilst this approach is important in understanding human behaviour in general, it is of relatively little value in explaining what motivates some students to study more than others.
>
> (Stapleton 2001:102)

This has little to offer education in terms of the motivation of pupils, although an empty stomach or dehydration can certainly affect classroom performance. The concepts of arousal and motivation are both physiological and psychological according to Lefrançois (1997). The former is related to how our heart rate, blood pressure, respiration and brainwave activity underpin our *alertness*. The latter element is related to the degree of alertness or attentiveness we display. For every task we undertake there is a level of arousal '*at which performance will be at its optimum*' (Lefrançois 1997: 102). When we are asleep, our arousal level is very low therefore our performance on a task is poor. Obviously it follows that trying to work when you are too tired will mean your performance is less effective. As we become more aroused, our performance on a task begins to be more effective, until we finally reach our optimum performance. There is a danger that if the levels of arousal continue to climb, to the levels of panic, then performance will fall.

> As individuals, we behave in ways which attempt to keep our level of arousal as close to that needed for optimum task performance as possible. If we find something boring, for example, we may daydream, thus increasing our level of arousal, and helping us to drift back to the task at hand. Conversely, if we are over-aroused, we may do something to reduce arousal, such as doodling on an exam paper to reduce the feeling of panic when we find that our mind has gone blank!
>
> (Ibid: 103)

Cognitive

One cognitive approach to motivation is visualisation whilst another looks at motivational traits. Both are concerned with how we consider our behaviour and the thought we put into planning and achieving goals. Kagan and Lang (1978) believe that we are capable of visualising future events through our thoughts, wishes and desires – cognitive representations. It is this ability to create a possible future that motivates us. We can work out what we want and what kind of behaviour will get us there or we can be motivated by the difference in our current 'reality' and the possible 'better future'. For the motivation to be successful we must be able to visualise the 'desired outcome'. Kagan and Lang propose that visualisation achieves its effects through the operation of one or more of six major needs or desires. See Figure 3. 3.

Figure 3.3 Kagan and Lang: major motives and desires

Major motive or desire	Examples of what teachers can do to allow these desires to be met and thus motivate students
Desire for approval from significant others	Establish an atmosphere in which both effort and quality work is seen as desirable by all
Desire to identify with others	Establish a relationship which fosters identification, by being a suitable role model ... prepared for every lesson, happy in their work, etc.
Desire for mastery	Set tasks that are achievable, but only after effort. Too easy tasks are as unmotivating as too difficult ones.
Desire to resolve uncertainty	Build up problem solving skills and set appropriate problems as part of class work
Desire for control, power and status	Encourage mutual respect, negotiate rather than impose deadlines for work completion (whenever possible)
Desire to vent hostility	Be willing to accept criticism from students when it is warranted

Trumper (1995) has identified four motivational traits:

1. achievement – broadly equivalent to 'desire for mastery'
2. curiosity – desire to resolve uncertainty
3. sociability – approval from significant others
4. conscientiousness – an element of approval from others

Task 3C

Consider what motivates you.
Can you analyse this using Kagan and Lang's or Trumper's theories?

Humanist

Abraham Maslow proposed 'that humans have a dual needs system that can be arranged in a hierarchical fashion' (1970: 105). Maslow maintained that the needs at the lower levels, the basic needs had to be at least, partially met before those at the upper levels became important motivators for behaviour. When basic needs for food and safety are threatened, the motivation to meet these needs is far more important than the desire to meet the needs of affiliation or affection. The ultimate state of being, once all others have been met in full or partially, is self-actualisation – being the most complete human one can be. Figure 3.4 outlines Maslow's Hierarchy of Needs.

Fgure 3.4 Maslow's Hierarchy of Needs

Self–actualisation
self-fulfillment realising one's potential
Aesthetic
truth justice goodness beauty symmetry
Cognitive
knowledge understanding exploration
Self-esteem
achievement recognition competence approval
Belongingness and love
affiliation trust acceptance affection
Safety
protection from danger security psychological safety
Physiological needs
food drink oxygen rest activity sex

(Based on Gross (1996) and Lefrançois (1997) in Stapleton 2001: 106)
Basic needs consist of the lower four elements of the 'pyramid': physiological needs, safety, belongingness and love and self-esteem
Meta-needs consist of the remaining three elements.

Task 3D

What relevance has Maslow's Hierarchy of Needs for
a) learners?
b) yourself?

In your response you may have identified the need to ensure that the classroom environment is safe, warm, friendly (where every individual is respected for who they are) and with the promise of stimulation – 'arousal' and reward. These will form a good foundation for motivating learners to be the best that they can be.

Intelligence – emotional and personal

Emotional intelligence

The term emotional literacy was coined by Claude Steiner (1935–) but developed significantly by Daniel Goleman. Goleman (1995) took the work of research psychologists such as Peter Salovey *et al.* (1997) and neuroscientists such as Joseph LeDoux (1986) and made it accessible to a wide public audience. Emotional literacy has also become know as emotional intelligence. Howard Gardner has been instrumental in the last 20 years in challenging the notion that intelligence is a single capacity. He proposes the existence of several 'intelligences' but for the purposes of this chapter we shall discuss 'intrapersonal' and 'interpersonal' intelligence. These are the two constituents of our overall 'emotional intelligence'.

The personal intelligences

As Gardner argues an understanding of personal intelligences is helpful in functioning within a wider community because it involves you in a greater understanding of other people. *Intrapersonal intelligence* is an intelligence that involves recognising your own emotions and the effects that others and situations have on you.

> In its most primitive form, the intrapersonal intelligence amounts to little more than the capacity to distinguish a feeling of pleasure from one of pain, on the basis of such discrimination, to become more involved in or to withdraw from a situation. At its most advanced level, intrapersonal knowledge allows one to detect and to symbolise complex and highly differentiated sets of feelings.
>
> (Gardner 1993: 239)

Interpersonal intelligence is the ability to detect these emotions of pleasure or pain in others and to use this information to advantage in achieving a desired aim.

> Examined in its most elementary form, the interpersonal intelligence entails the capacity of the young child to discriminate among the individuals around him and to detect their various moods. In an advanced form, interpersonal knowledge permits

a skilled adult to read the intentions and desires – even when these are hidden – of many individuals and, potentially, to act upon this knowledge – for example, by influencing a group of disparate individuals to behave along desired lines. We see highly developed forms of interpersonal intelligence in political and religious leaders, in skilled parents and teachers, and in individuals enrolled in the helping professions, be they therapists, counsellors, or shamans.

(Ibid: 239)

Emotional hijacks

An emotional hijack may happen to every one of us every day. An emotional hijack occurs when we lose control as our emotions take over. We may hit out if we don't understand and retaliate using inappropriate behaviour. Emotional hijacks frustrate adults and children and can lead to a downward spiral of negative self-esteem. The hijack happens because the brain has not yet developed to the point where the emotional response can be connected to the thinking brain, enabling us to plan the most appropriate way to behave in the situation. Instead the fast, survival-based connections in the brain rush reflexively into action. We can however, learn to connect the thinking brain to the reaction through experiences and interactions with adults. It is important therefore, not only to manage the hijacks but also to develop empathy and the ability to manage other people's emotional states. Salovey and Mayer (1990) concluded that these attributes are critically important to being effective in the world.

So in order to operate effectively in the communities within which we function there are a number of issues to consider:

- We can be taught how to respond less on impulse and more on reason – managing the hijacks
- Learning takes place through appropriate experiences and interactions
- We need to be able to 'empathise', or identify with others
- The ability to manage other people's emotional states is important
- These skills can be learned in an environment that holds appropriate attitudes and values to underpin them.

Task 3E

Think about the workplace and identify opportunities that may be provided for learners to address:

- Recognising their own emotions
- Understanding and expressing them appropriately – possibly through modelling and role play
- Recognising the emotions of others – learning to read facial expressions, tones of voice
- Understanding how others might feel
- Responding in appropriate ways to other people's emotions

The brain is very important in learning, not just as storage and processing device for facts but as we have seen it can also affect our emotional state and ability to learn effectively. In the next section we consider the link between exercise, nutrition and brain development.

Physical exercise, nutrition and brain development

The brain is amazing. We have four brains in one, situated on three distinct levels with the fourth tucked in behind. There are two sides which control different functions and process information in different ways. These sides are linked by an electronic- and chemical-relay system which shuttles information around instantly. We have many different 'intelligence centres', but very few of us develop more than a small part of that latent ability. The brain has at least four different electrical wavelengths, like different TV channels. The most advanced part of the brain has six distinct layers. We have an active conscious brain and a subconscious brain.

To put it simply the *lower brain or brain stem* controls many of our instincts, such as breathing and heartbeat. This segment is almost identical to that of a lizard's, crocodile's or bird's brain and for this reason it has been called the 'reptilian' brain. It controls the instinct to 'fight or flight'. The *central part of the brain* controls the emotions. This is known as the *limbic* system and is often called the 'old mammalian' brain, because it is similar to the brains of other mammals. It's the part of the brain that is programmed to instruct a baby to suckle almost instantly at birth. It is our emotional and sexual centre and is connected with parts of the brain that deal with memory storage. Amazingly, we can often remember things better when we have an emotional connection to them. The *upper brain* enables us to think, talk, reason and create. This two-sided cerebrum is capped by, what looks like, a crumpled blanket known as the *cortex*. The 'crumpled blanket' is only about 3 millimetres thick, but has six layers which have different functions. It also has several distinct centres, to process input from individual senses and react to them. It is the part of the brain that makes us distinct from any other living creature. Tucked in at the back is the *cerebellum*. This plays a vital role in storing 'muscle memory': the things we remember by actively performing tasks, such as riding a bike or playing football. It also plays a key role in adjusting posture and balance, but more recently its importance in learning and for speech has been discovered.

The two sides of your brain, the left hemisphere and the right hemisphere, are linked by the *corpus callosum*. It is generally known that the left-hand side is responsible for processing logic, words, mathematics and sequence – the so-called academic parts of learning. The right-hand side deals with rhythm, rhyme, music, pictures and day-dreaming – the so-called creative activities. But this is a major over-simplification. The corpus callosum, which links the two, is a highly complex switching system that is constantly balancing the incoming messages and linking together the abstract, holistic picture with the concrete, logical messages.

Our brains are dynamic. They can change at any age, from birth right through to the end of life. That change can be positive if one is exposed to stimulating environments, or it can be negative if not exposed to stimulation.

> Your brain is made up of a trillion brain cells. Each brain cell is like the most phenomenal complex little octopus. It has a centre, it has many branches, and each branch has many connection points. Each one of those billions of brain cells is many times more powerful and sophisticated than most of the computers around the

planet today. Each one of these cells connects, embraces, hundreds of thousands to tens of thousands of others. And they shuttle information back and forward. It's been called an enchanted look, the most astoundingly complex, beautiful thing in existence. And each person has one.

(Dryden and Vos 2001: 114–15)

Development and language

The ability to process linguistic messages rapidly – a prerequisite for the understanding of normal speech – seems to depend upon the integrity of the left temporal lobe. In right-handed individuals language is linked to the operation of certain areas in the left hemisphere of the brain. Injuries to the normal development of this neural zone often lead to language impairments. This may lead to problems in comprehension but also in speech articulation. If, however, an area as large as an entire hemisphere of the brain is removed during the first year of life, a child will still be able to speak quite well. Early in life the brain is capable of being supple and language is sufficiently important to enable it to develop in the right hemisphere at the cost of compromising visual and special functions that would normally be localised there. When a person's language development is impaired through damage to the left hemisphere children will be dependent upon the analytical mechanisms of the right hemisphere and will use semantic information to decode sentences. They will rely on meanings of main words and may acquire language at a slower rate. Some linguistic mechanisms are located in quite distinct regions of the brain. The syntactic processes are mediated by the Broca's area; others are more widely dispersed in the left hemisphere of the brain, such as the semantic system. Others are dependent upon right hemisphere structures, such as the pragmatic functions of language. With age, these functions become increasingly focalized in normal right-handed individuals: the more complex interactions depend upon a flow of information within these linguistic regions.

Brain strengthening

There are many exercises we can do that strengthen the brain and the way in which it works. Try some of these!

Brain buttons

You need to stand and find your collar bone. With your first finger and thumb of one hand, find the space between your first and second rib, down from your collar bone, either side of your breast bone. The other hand needs to be held over your navel. Massage the two points with your finger and thumb while the other hand is held over the navel. Move your eyes from side to side as smoothly as you can. This helps to re-establish the organisation necessary for skills used in reading and writing.

The cross crawl

This involves moving one arm and its opposite leg. Touch your elbow of the right arm with the raised knee of the left leg. Then repeat with the left elbow and right knee. Repeat between five and ten times. Alternatively you can do the cross crawl from a lying down position. This movement activates left/right, top/bottom, and back/front areas of the brain and the body simultaneously.

Hook ups

This can be done sitting down, standing or lying down. Part one: cross left ankle over the right, or vice versa. Extend arms in front of you, left wrist over right (or vice versa) and thumbs down, palms together. Interlace fingers and draw hands close to the chest, elbows down. (As you pull your arms to your chest you will have to roll your hands down, under and up to be able to hold them to your chest). Now rest the tongue on the roof of the mouth behind the teeth and breathe in and out. Part two: unhook the feet and hands and place the fingertips together and feet flat on the floor for a few seconds. This has a calming and stress-relieving effect.

Brain food

Dryden and Vos (2001) remind us that the brain is like a complex machine that requires energy which it gets from the food we eat. As an adult our brain makes up only about 2 per cent of our total weight. But it uses about 20 per cent of the energy we develop. For energy, the brain needs plenty of glucose. That's why fresh fruit and vegetables which are rich in glucose are essential. The brain transmits messages around the body both chemically and electrically, and it keeps switching from one to another. The brain controls the flow of these transmitters. It requires both good food and oxygen. We get oxygen through breathing which is why exercise and deep breathing are important before and during study. Try incorporating some of these foods into your own diet to improve brain function.

- Lecithin-rich food for memory – peanuts, soya beans and wheat germ
- Linoleic acid to increase mental performance – polyunsaturated fats such as corn oil, fish
- Iron-rich foods for mental performance
- Sodium and potassium supply the pumps which transmit all the brain's messages – bananas, oranges, avocados, melons, potatoes, tomatoes and others are all potassium rich, sodium is found in most foods

The brain is composed of almost 90 per cent water, and needs to be kept hydrated.

The effect of the environment on the brain

The brain operates on four main frequencies, Alpha, Beta, Delta and Theta waves. The optimum state of mind for 'deep learning' is when your brain is in a state of relaxed alertness. This is the 'alpha' wave. If you are wide awake and alert at the moment, you are operating in the 'beta' level. This is not the best level to be operating in as it is not a state that stimulates your long-term memory. It does, however, get you through the day, but inhibits access to the deeper levels of the mind. Most of the information you learn will be stored in your subconscious mind. During a state of 'relaxed alertness' in the 'alpha' level, you are able to reach your subconscious and therefore learning will be 'long-term'. As you get sleepier, during the 'twilight zone' between being awake and fully asleep, your mind processes the day's information; this is the 'theta' level. Deep sleep takes you into the 'delta' level. Although you do not want to be in theta or delta, to be able to learn faster, you need periods where you slow your brain down.

Much recent research has been built on the work of the Bulgarian psychiatrist Lozanov (see Lozanov 1978). His disciples have concluded after years of research that

> we each have an optimum learning state ... where heartbeat, breathing and brainwaves are smoothly synchronised and the body is relaxed but the mind concentrated and ready to receive new information.
>
> (Dryden and Vos 2001)

The effect of background music on task performance

There is strong evidence that people respond differently to stimulating and sedative music, but much of the research on effects of music on behaviour and cognitive processing is relatively unsystematic and inconclusive.

> This is in part, because music can be processed in different ways. While there may be general trends in our responses to stimulating or relaxing music, these are overlaid by individual cognitions which may mediate the immediate effects, for instance, associations of particular pieces of music with particular events or dislike of particular musical genres.
>
> (Hallam *et al.* 2000: 111–12)

However, music in adolescence has a great cultural importance (North *et al.*, 2000). In addition, Scott (1970) noted that children with special educational needs could be calmed with music and that mathematical performance improved. Hallam and Price (1998) found similar effects of music on children with emotional and behavioural difficulties. In addition several studies have reported a music-induced decrease in activity level in ADHD (attention-deficit/hyperactivity disorder) children (Cripe 1986) and mentally retarded children (Gregoire 1984; Reardon and Bell 1970), while Savan (1998) has demonstrated improved behaviour and a greater concentration on school work when Mozart was played during the science lessons of ten children with learning, emotional and behavioural difficulties. Nevertheless, music can disrupt those who struggle to concentrate as their attention becomes focussed on it rather than on their work. In addition positive effects can diminish with growing familiarity over time (Hallam *et al.* 2002).

Task 3F

Thinking about what we have learned about the brain, how do you think information like this has influenced or should influence education?

In your opinion how could the curriculum be modified to provide opportunities to promote physical exercise, healthy eating?

When should we begin to educate learners about diet and exercise?

Who else needs access to this kind of information?

Schooling and cognitive development

Schools are causally linked to the emergence of some advanced cognitive skills. Studies have shown that 'schooling exposes children to many specific skills and types of knowledge and appears to stimulate the development of more flexible, generalised strategies for remembering and solving problems' (Bee 2000: 413). School should be seen as a complex social environment. Encouraging parental involvement to help motivate children and help them adapt to school life is important. Schools offer parents help in understanding ways in which they can help their children learn and develop and this practice will develop a stronger sense of community. (Bee 2000)

   Task 3G

How can education meet the challenge of ensuring maximum cognitive development for all learners?

We must acknowledge that schools today are at the heart of their communities; however, this can be a source of tension as Gardner (1991) has identified.

> Just as the mind of the five-year-old endures in the school-age pupil, so too the values and practices of the wider community do not disappear just because the student happens to be sitting in class and listening to the teacher talk.
>
> (Gardner 1991: 127–39)

Conclusion

This chapter has attempted to summarise some of the key ideas about growth, development and learning. This is quite a difficult task and we have had to be selective in our choice of information. Nevertheless, we have looked at the ways in which children are nurtured and at how they might be motivated. We have looked at the processes of learning and have considered how the brain functions and the impact that environment, nutrition and exercise have on cognitive abilities. It would be interesting to consider how all of this information links to the setting within which you work. How effective is the environment in supporting the learning needs of your learners? If you would like to extend your reading in this area look through the following reference section.

📖 Bibliography

Bandura, A. (1973) *Aggression: A Social Learning Analysis*. Englewood Cliffs, NJ: Prentice Hall.

Bandura, A. (1977) *Social Learning Theory*. Englewood Cliffs, NJ: Prentice Hall.

Bandura, A. (1982) 'Self-efficacy mechanism in human agency', *American Psychologist*, 37, 122–47.

Bandura, A. (1986) *Social Foundations of Thought and Action: A Social Cognitive Theory*. Englewood Cliffs, NJ: Prentice Hall.

Bandura, A. (1989) 'Social cognitive theory', *Annals of Child Development*, 6, 1–60.

Bandura, A. (1997) *Self-efficacy: The Exercise of control*. New York: Freeman.

Baumrind, D (1973) 'The development of Instrumental competence through socialisation' in Pick A.D. (ed.) *Minnesota Symposium on Child Psychology* (Vol 7) Minneapolis, MN: University of Minneapolis.

Boyes, M.C. and Allen, S.G. (1993) 'Styles of parent–child interactions and moral reasoning in adolescence', *Merrill-Palmer Quarterly*, 39, 551–70.

Bee, H. (2000) *The Developing Child*, 9th edn, Boston, MA: Allyn & Bacon.

Biggs, J.B. and Moore, P.J. (1993) *The Process of Learning* 3rd edn, New York: Prentice Hall.

Bruner, J.S. (1975) 'The ontogenesis of speech act', *Journal of Child Language*, 2, 1–21.

Bruner, J.S. (1976) 'Learning to do things with words' in Bruner, J.S. and Garton, A. (eds) *Human Growth and Development*, Oxford: Oxford University Press.

Carr, R., Light, P. and Woodhead, M. (1991) *Child Development in Social Context 3. Growing up in a Changing Society*, London: Open University Press, Routledge.

Chomsky, N. (1965) *Aspects of a Theory of Syntax*. Cambridge, MA: MIT Press.

Chomsky, N. (1975) *Reflections on Language*, New York: Pantheon Books.

Chomsky, N. (1986) *Knowledge of Language: Its Nature, Origin, and Use*, New York: Praeger.

Chomsky, N. (1988) *Language and Problems of Knowledge*. Cambridge, MA: MIT Press.

Cripe, F.F. (1986): 'Rock music as therapy for children with attention deficit disorder; an exploratory study', *Journal of Music Therapy*, 23(10), 30–7.

Donaldson, M (1986) *Children's Minds*, Oxford: Blackwell.

Dryden, G. and Vos, J. (2001) *The Learning Revolution*, Auckland: Network Educational Press.

Freud, S. (1905) *The Basic Writings of Sigmund Freud* (trans. A.A. Brill), New York: Random House.

Freud, S. (1920) *A General Introduction to Psychoanalysis* (trans. J. Riviere), New York: Washington Square Press.

Gardner, H. (1993) *Frames of Mind*, 10th anniversary edn, New York: Basic Books.

Gardner, H. (1991) *The Unschooled Mind*, New York: Basic Books.

Girogian, N.A. (1974) 'Pavlov, Ivan Petrovich', in *The Dictionary of Scientific Biography*, vol 10, New York: Charles Schribner & Sons.

Glasgow, K.L., Dornbusch, S.M., Troyer, L., Steinberg, L. and Ritter, P.L. (1997) 'Parenting styles, adolescents' attributions, and educational outcomes in nine heterogeneous high schools', *Child Development*, 68(3), 507–29.

Goleman, D. (1995). *Emotional Intelligence*, New York: Bantam Books.

Gregoire, M.A. (1984) 'Music as a prior condition to task performance', *Journal of Music Therapy*, 21, 133–45.

Gross, J. (1996) *Special Educational Needs in the Primary School*, Buckingham: Open University Press.

Hallam, S. and Price, J. (1998) 'Can the use of background music improve the behaviour and academic performance of children with emotional and behavioural difficulties?', *British Journal of Special Education*, 25(2), 88–91.

Hallam, S., Price, J. and Katsarou, G. (2002) 'Issues relating to environment: effects of background music on task performance', *Educational Studies*, 28(2).

James, W. (1890) *Principles of Psychology*, Chicago, IL: Encyclopaedia Britannica.

James, W. (1892) *Psychology: The Briefer Course*, New York: Holt.

Kagan, J. and Lang, C. (1978) *Psychology and Education*, New York: Harcourt.

Kozulin, A. (1984) 'Personalities and reflexes: the legacies of Ivan Pavlov and Vladimir Bekterev', in *Psychology in Utopia: Toward a Social History of Soviet Psychology*, Cambridge, MA: MIT Press.

Lang, P.J., Bradley, M.M. and Cuthbert, B.N. (1992) 'A motivational analysis of emotion: reflex-cortex connections', *Psychological Science*, 3, 44–9.

LeDoux, J.E. (1986) 'The neurobiology of emotion', in LeDoux, J.E. and Hirst, W. (eds) *Mind and Brain: Dialogues in Cognitive Neuroscience*, New York: Read.

Lee, V. and Gupta, P.D. (1995) *Children's Cognitive and Language Development*, Buckingham: Open University Press/Blackwell.

Lefrançois, G.R. (1997) *Psychology for Teaching*, 9th edn, Belmont, CA: Wadsworth.

Lozanov, G. (1982) 'Suggestology and suggestopedy' in Blair, R. (ed.) *Innovative approaches to Language Teaching*, Rowley, MA: Newbury House.

Maccoby, E.E. and Martin, J.A (1983) 'Socialization in the context of the family: parent–child interaction', in Hetherington, E.M. (ed.) *Handbook of Child Psychology: Socialisation, Personality and Social Development*, Vol 4, New York: Wiley.

McGuire, J. and Richman N. (1986) 'The prevalence of behaviour problems in three types of preschool group', *Journal of Child Psychology & Psychiatry*, 27, 455–72.

Maslow, A. (1998) *Toward a Psychology of Being*, 3rd edn, New York: Wiley.

Maslow, A. (1970) *Motivation and Personality*, 3rd edn, New York: Harper.

Maslow, A. (1971) *The Further Reaches of Human Nature*, Harmondworth: Penguin Books.

Melhuish, E.C., Mooney, A., Martin, S. and Lloyd, E. (1990a) 'Type of childcare at 18 months: I. Differences in interactional experience', *Journal of Child Psychology & Psychiatry*, 31(6).

Melhuish, E.C., Mooney, A., Martin, S. and Lloyd, E. (1990b) 'Type of childcare at 18 months: II. Relations with cognitive and language development', *Journal of Child Psychology & Psychiatry*, 31(6).

North, A.C., Hargreaves, D.J. and O'Neill, S.A. (2000) 'The importance of music to adolescents', *British Journal of Educational Psychology*, 70, 255–72.

Oxford Dictionary of Current English (1985) Oxford: Oxford University Press.

Pavlov, I. (1926) *Conditioned Reflexes* (trans. and ed. by G.V. Anrep) London: Oxford University Press.

Piaget, J. (1932) *The Moral Judgment of the Child*, New York: Macmillan.

Piaget, J. (1952) *The Origins of Intelligence in Children*, New York: International Universities Press.

Piaget, J. (1954) [1937] *The Construction of Reality in the Child*, New York: Basic Books.

Piaget, J. (1970) 'Piaget's theory', in Mussen, P.H. (ed.), *Carmichael's Manual of Child Psychology*, New York: Wiley.

Piaget, J. (1977) *The Development of Thought: Equilibration of Cognitive Structures*, New York: Viking Press.

Pittman, L.D. and Chase-Lansdale, P.L. (2001) 'African-American adolescent girls in impoverished communities: parenting style and adolescent outcomes', *Journal of Research on Adolescence*, 11: 199–24.

Reardon D.M. and Bell G. (1970) 'Effects of sedative and stimulative music on activity levels of severely retarded boys', *American Journal of Mental Deficiency*, 75(2), 156–9.

Salovey, P. and Mayer, J. (1990) 'Emotional intelligence', *Imagination, Cognition, and Personality*, 9(3), 185–211.

Salovey, P. and Sluyter, D. (1997) *Emotional Development and Emotional Intelligence: Implications for Educators*, New York: Basic Books.

Savan, A. (1998) 'A study of the effect of background music on the behaviour and physiological responses of children with special educational needs', *The Psychology of Education Review*, 22(1), 32–5.

Savan, A. (1999) 'The effect of background music on learning', *Psychology of Music*, 27, 138–46.

Scott, T. (1970) 'The use of music to reduce hyperactivity in children', *American Journal of Orthopsychiatry*, 4, 677–80.

Stapleton, M. (2001) *Psychology in Practice: Education*, London: Hodder and Stoughton.

Sylva, K. and Lunt, I. (1982) *Child Development: A First Course*, Oxford: Blackwell.

Trumper, R, (1995) 'Students' motivational traits in science: a cross-age study', *British Educational Research Journal*, 21, 505–15.

Vygotsky, L.S. (1962) *Thought and Language*, New York: Wiley.

Vygotsky, L.S. (1967) 'Play and its role in the mental development of the child', *Soviet Psychology*, 5, 6–18.

Vygotsky, L.S. (1978) *Mind and Society: The Development of Higher Mental Processes*, Cambridge, MA: Harvard University Press.

Chapter 4

The development of language and literacy

In this chapter we look at what it is to be literate, providing you with an overview of the myriad pieces of information available about the development of language and literacy skills. We will explore the importance of learning through talk, looking at the types of communication strategies available. We consider the acquisition, function and importance of speaking and listening, reading and writing skills and the impact they have on developing learning. We show how stories can be used to underpin the development of many forms of literacy and we include a brief analysis of the barriers that can delay language acquisition. Alongside this we consider the ways in which learners can be supported by teaching assistants and look at the key vehicle for the teaching of language in schools – The Literacy Hour.

Language and literacy in the curriculum

The key skill of communication includes skills in speaking, listening, reading and writing. Skills in speaking and listening include the ability to speak effectively for different audiences; to listen, understand and respond appropriately to others; and to participate effectively in group discussion. Skills in reading and writing include the ability to read fluently a range of literary and non-fiction texts and to reflect critically on what is read; the ability to write fluently for a range of purposes and audiences, including critical analysis of their own and others' writing.

(DfES 1999)

The National Literacy Strategy introduced in 1998 provides a Framework for Teaching. It sets out teaching objectives for Reception to Year 6 to enable pupils to become fully literate. Even if you are not involved with this age group it is important to understand the principls of early literacy. The Literacy Hour is intended to promote literacy instruction. The most successful teaching is identified as that which is discursive. It is characterised by:

➤ High quality oral work
➤ Interactive teaching where pupils' contributions are encouraged, expected and extended
➤ Well-paced lessons with a sense of urgency, driven by the need to make progress and succeed

➤ Confident teachers who have a clear understanding of the objectives
➤ Optimism about and high expectations of success.

Task 4A

Which of the listed items relate to the role of teaching assistant?
How can teaching assistants work with teachers to ensure successful teaching and learning of literacy whatever the age of the learner?

The Literacy Strategy is underpinned by the theories of Vygotsky and Bruner, which focus attention on the interactive process of teaching and learning and are particularly concerned with social discourse, collaborative learning and the joint construction of knowledge. They highlight the importance of effective teacher intervention and scaffolding strategies, such as modelling and demonstrating. The learner is envisaged as an apprentice, initially requiring a great deal of support and gradually becoming more proficient, finally being able to operate independently. The concept of scaffolding is important and particularly useful because it neither places teachers firmly within an instructional, transmission role, nor marginalises them, but 'represents both teacher and learner as active participants in the construction of knowledge' (Mercer 1995: 74).

Developing language: the role of language in learning

> As language develops it acts like a sculptor, carving into ever-sharper relief the features of the objective human world.
>
> (DeLaguna 1927: 274).

Language is a system for understanding which is shared and communicated between at least two people. It is a way that humans convey information, intentionally or unintentionally. There are three main theories of how language is learned: behaviourist, nativist and social interactionist.

The *behaviourist* theory has its roots in the thinking of philosopher Locke (1632–1704) who believed that infants are born with 'a blank sheet' knowing nothing. As a consequence people are the sum total of what they learn as they grow older. Behavioural psychologists consider that language is behaviour to be learned just like other behaviours. They suggest that language is developed through imitating sounds and through making noises that caregivers 'shape' until they become words. The *nativist* view is connected with the American linguist Chomsky (1928–). His studies gave him an understanding of the complexities of language. He considered that for a child to learn the complex rule systems of language they must be born with some of this knowledge already in place. Infants then adapt this knowledge to suit the particular language community they are born into. This enables very young children to learn other languages very easily at this stage. The *social interactionist* view emphasises the connections between speaker and listener. The American psychologist Bruner (1915–) emphasises the connections that exist in pre-verbal exchanges between child and caregiver and its importance for later language development (Bruner 1975). These pre-verbal exchanges have the structure of conversations such as turn taking. In this shared exchange the child's partner in the communication makes the greatest contribution until the child is able to take a more active role.

Both behaviourist and nativist theories place the child as a 'passive' player in the developmental process. Studies have shown however, that even before the acquisition of language, the sounds infants make communicate their intentions proving them to be an active contributor (Bates *et al.* 1975). Bruner (1976) argues that the developmental process progresses as the child and adult become equally responsible for giving and receiving. Lee and Gupta (1995) make the distinction between receptive language and productive language, those words that a learner can understand and those that they can produce. The development of vocabulary is slow at first and varies somewhat. Nonetheless, learners are likely to have a vocabulary of about 50 words by 18 or 20 months of age.

Wray and Medwell (1991) suggest that the pattern of discourse in schools is that of Initiation – Response – Feedback. The cycle consists of three 'moves', typically the teacher asks a question, a pupil volunteers an answer and the teacher evaluates that answer. This is a transmission approach to learning where classrooms are dominated by the teacher speaking and questioning that demands recall to answer. There is, however, an alternative or additional approach to learning and teaching that involves recognising the importance of what the learner brings to the classroom, the interpretation approach. This is summarised in Figure 4.1.

Vygotsky (1978), called for pedagogy where discourse plays a central role in the formulation of meaning. He believed that the mind is ever active, providing a constant internal dialogue or 'stream of consciousness' and offering a critical evaluation of life around us. This 'private talk' allows us to think in abstractions, dig out memories and project future events. For Vygotsky 'every function in the child's cultural development appears twice: first on the social level and later on the individual level' (1978: 57). Vygotsky believed that cognitive mechanisms are generated in a social context so that learners interact with other people as they are learning, which not only provides a richer source of input, but also makes possible particular kinds of learning. Bruner offers a useful summary of the concept:

> If the child is enabled to advance by being under the tutelage of an adult or a more competent peer, then the tutor of the aiding peer serves the learner as a vicarious form of consciousness until such a time as the learner is able to master his own action through his own consciousness and control. When the child achieves that conscious control over a new function or conceptual system, it is then that he is able to use it as a tool. Up to that point, the tutor in effect performs the critical function of scaffolding

Figure 4.1 Transmission and interpretation models

Transmission	Interpretation
Learners seen as empty vessels	Existing knowledge is recognised
Teacher determines what is taught	Learning needs determine what is taught
Teacher transmits information	Learning needs determine what is taught
Asymmetric discourse pattern	Interactive discourse pattern
Learners passively receive information	Learners interpret and actively evaluate information

the learning task to make it possible for the child, in Vygotsky's words, to internalise external knowledge and convert it into a tool for conscious control.

(Bruner 1986: 24–5)

Knowledge reformulated by the learner is more easily recalled, linked to other knowledge, and so accessible from other points in thought. This makes it more easily used in daily living, or when solving a problem. Knowledge that the learner does not reformulate is more readily forgotten and only recalled in similar situations to which it was learned. This type of knowledge is difficult to apply. The Assessment of Performance Unit (APU) (1988: 5) identified a number of purposes of talk in school and recognised the learning potential of collaborative discussions where learners evaluate, speculate, expound and hypothesise.

Cooperation is working together to accomplish shared goals and cooperative learning is the instructional use of small groups so that students work together to maximise their own and one another's learning.

(Johnson and Johnson 1990: 69)

Psychologists and theorists have stressed the role of talk in organising our understanding of the world. Language both structures and directs the processes of thinking (Vygotsky 1965). Learners working together are able to develop and recall solutions to problems that, alone, they would not be able to resolve (Light and Glachan 1985). Piaget (1954) argued that some knowledge and experience can be 'assimilated' because it fits comfortably into our existing schemes for understanding the world, and that other new ideas, because they do not fit, force us to 'accommodate' them by changing our schemes. Wells (1987) has identified how learners use talk to 'make meaning' of their experiences. They engage with others in collaborative action and in the co-construction of meaning. This process actively transforms the information they have received. The learner's resulting knowledge is never a straightforward copy, but a new, personal, reconstruction of knowledge.

Ways of communicating

Communication is a two-way process and is made up of three parts. There is the source of the message, the content of the message and then the receiver of the message. These three elements interact in different ways resulting in a variety of communication styles that vary in effectiveness dependent on the character of the communication and the way in which it is received. Atkinson (1992) believes that it is important to consider these issues of comprehension and the channels of communication utilised. There are three main ways in which we communicate:

➤ Non-verbal communication (NVC)
➤ Speaking and listening
➤ Reading and writing.

Non-verbal communication

Non-verbal communication (NVC) has several different functions. It allows us to express emotion through the use of our face, body, and voice. Argyle (1983) has identified six emotional expressions – happiness, surprise, fear, sadness, anger and disgust/contempt. These non-verbal signals are an essential part of communicating interpersonal attitudes. We develop and sustain relationships by using signals, such as proximity, facial expression, voice tone, touch and gaze. As Abercrombie (1968) argued we may speak with our vocal organs but we converse with our whole body. We use non-verbal signals to accompany and support speech and engage in a complex sequence of non-verbal vocalisations, such as hand gestures and head movements. We present powerful images of ourselves and shape our identity through non-verbal communication. Many professions have an unwritten dress code (Malloy 1977). This is because we communicate many aspects of self through our appearance. We also give messages about ourselves through our voice and the way we modulate sounds. Argyle (1983) argues that the correct use of NVC is an essential part of social competence and of specific social skills. Such considerations are important when working with children or young adults in education.

Not only do we communicate with our bodies and gestures but we communicate through the way in which we set up a learning environment. For example, a classroom layout should be planned in advance to express the teacher's expectations for the lesson. Both distance and orientation of the pupils in relation to the teacher can affect the quality of interaction (Argyle 1983; Neill and Caswell 1993). Neill and Caswell (1993) argued that the personal, social and public distances between the teacher and students as they move around the classroom was important. For example, the closer the teacher is to the student the stronger the message. In addition, the position of the teacher's desk can hinder communication if it presents a physical barrier. A lack of visual contact with a learner can make them feel distant from the teacher and in seating arrangements where learners are side facing they may not feel inclined to contribute actively to the lesson. Barnes (1976) found that small groups of four were most conducive for talk where learners can learn from and with each other in discussing and talking around shared experiences, without self-consciousness and with co-operative effort.

 Task 4B

Consider your working environment.
Are there any NVC barriers to communication and if so, how could they be counteracted?
Think about the learners you support.
How do you encourage effective communication between yourself and the learners?
How do you encourage communication between learners in the group?

Speaking and listening

How we talk is greatly influenced by the immediate context in which we find ourselves (Barnes 1992). Learners can be silenced by uncertainty about what is expected of them in the classroom. How learners talk depends both on their experiences inside and outside of the learning environment. Each environment uses talk for different purposes and there are different roles and rules associated with the language being used. In this country this is more difficult to access for those whose first language is not English. Learning to talk is part of learning to be a member of a particular culture (Wells 1989). Language should be viewed as a tool that the learner can use to bring order to their experiences (Bruner 1966). Barnes (1992) identified a four-staged model in order to use talk to support learning:

➤➤ *The focusing stage* encourages learners to verbalise the necessary preliminary knowledge.
➤➤ *The exploratory stage* allows learners to carry out the necessary manipulations of materials and talk about key issues in relation to the topic.
➤➤ *The reorganising stage* allows the teacher to refocus attention.
➤➤ *The public stage* at which knowledge is shared eventually leading to new discussion (Barnes 1976). Learners are most likely to develop their speaking and listening skills when they are struggling to say something important to them to someone who wants to hear.

By participating in, listening to and observing learners those teaching can assess the extent of support they need to give as well as identify other relevant activities that will develop understandings (Baddeley 1992). Those supporting learning can play several roles in supporting and encouraging talk for learning. They can act as an enabler, providing confidence and encouragement to use talk, or act as a role model for speaking or listening. They can also scaffold learning, becoming an active participant in the learning process. Questioning has a key role in supporting learning, motivating, sustaining and directing the thought processes of the learner. There are three types of questions that can be helpful when supporting reading and writing.

➤➤ Looking back questions: Can you tell me how you did that?
➤➤ Looking forward questions: Can you tell me how you will do that?
➤➤ Thinking aloud questions: What are you thinking as you are doing that?

We need to ensure that we use open questions that enable learners to engage with ideas rather than closed questions that demand and receive only short, factual responses. Allowing learners to formulate their own questions motivates them and can also indicate levels of understanding. Questions are not the only way of promoting talk. Wood (1991) identified alternatives such as telling, speculating, suggesting, negotiating and listening. Active listening is an important sophisticated skill which is different from social listening. It involves taking in what is being said, reflecting upon the message and then checking what is meant. An active listener supports what the speaker is saying and doesn't dominate with his or her own thoughts or experiences. Active listeners can demonstrate that they are listening by disagreeing with or by offering constructive criticisms of the issues raised. Poor listeners are likely to demonstrate traits such as interrogating, interrupting, ordering, warning, moralising, humiliating, being sarcastic, preaching or blaming.

The importance of speaking and listening for learning, and as a means of communication is explicitly and implicitly recognised in the National Curriculum. The Programme of Study for Speaking and Listening makes up one third of the National Curriculum for English. In addition the National Literacy Strategy text-level objectives require learners to discuss, evaluate, tell, explain, reason, summarise, and so forth. We have known for many years that talk is fundamental to a learner's development and learning. However teachers do not find it easy to engage learners in talk, particularly talk that challenges them to think for themselves (Ofsted 20020. The DfES (2003) document, *Excellence and Enjoyment: A Strategy for Primary Schools* highlights the role of the adult in the classroom as an active one. The teacher should model appropriate speaking and listening, including their role as a supportive and probing listener; they will encourage sensitive interaction and they should ensure goals are set with clear criteria for success.

Reading and writing

> People who grow up in a literate environment where reading and writing are naturally occurring daily activities have a distinct advantage when they start their formal education.

> (Wells 1986:194)

Early literacy is visible in children's understanding that signs and writing are systems of symbols that mean something. They see print on clothing, food packaging and environmental print both within and outside of the home. They see adults follow instructions on packages, reading and reacting to newspapers, magazines, bills, letters and using signs to find their way.

 Task 4C

Reflect on your own experience of learning to read.
What skills were taught and how were they taught?
Are you a good reader?
List the skills you need to be a reader?

Reading

Meek (1991) sees reading as a process by which readers re-create experience, extend it, think about it and possibly resist it. Because readers bring their own experience to the act of reading literacy is not the same for everyone. If reading is not the same for everyone we have to accommodate differences that exist between readers such as those based on gender, age, culture and class. To be able to read and to be a reader are not exactly the same things. The ability to read for practical ends differs from the reading that readers enjoy, the kind that makes them addicted to reading. If reading is a personal construct, then readers need to have the power to select their own reading material (Meek 1991). Before selection can be made, books must be available and accessible. This requires a positive reading environment (Chambers 1991). Chambers outlines three aspects that can be addressed to promote reading. The first is an inviting display that has a good selection of books and an arrangement designed to attract learners so that they will want to know more about books. The second is a designated reading area, a place devoted to one special activity,

Figure 4.2 A bottom-up model

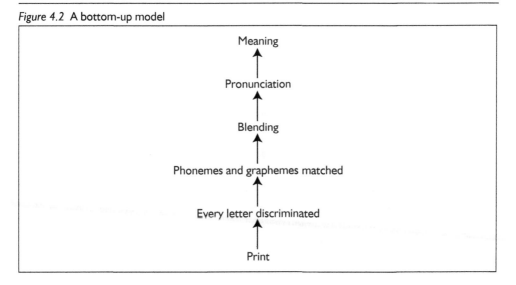

which signifies its value. Finally, being a reader means reading for oneself. The provision of Reading Time gives purpose to all other reading-based activities.

Some models of the reading process assume that the process starts with the recognition and decoding of letters, clusters of letters and words, with the reader processing progressively larger units of print up to the level of the sentence, paragraph, page and finally the complete text. These bottom-up models see reading as a process that begins outside the reader, whose task it is to transfer into his consciousness the meaning represented by the writer as graphic symbols. This is represented in Figure 4.2.

This shows the progression from recognising words as visual patterns to a more analytic approach. Frith (1985) outlined this progression and claimed that it was closely linked to spelling development. The first stage is the logographic stage; the learner treats words as logographs, recognising them by looking for salient features. The learner has no way of deciphering new words, except guessing if the word is in context. At the alphabetic stage the learner begins to learn letter-to-sound correspondence, and acquires the ability to decode unfamiliar words. At the orthographic stage the learner can identify words by making use of larger orthographic units and analogies between such units, without the need for grapheme-to-phoneme conversion. For example, they might learn to use larger spelling patterns, such as 'ight' and 'ing'.

In a whole-word approach to reading development, the overall shape and gross visual features of the word are stressed, not the component letters. Learners are taught to recognise a small set of words, each of which is displayed singly on a card called a flashcard. Alternatively, top-down models propose that the reading process begins in the mind of the reader who hypothesises about the meaning of the print to be read. The reader then samples the text to confirm or reject these hypotheses. Reading therefore does not require the processing of every letter or even of every word, but only sufficient of the text to allow the reader to gain an impression of its meaning. The most significant feature of reading is what is brought to the text from within the reader's mind. Figure 4.3 illustrates a top-down model of reading development.

Figure 4.3 A top-down model

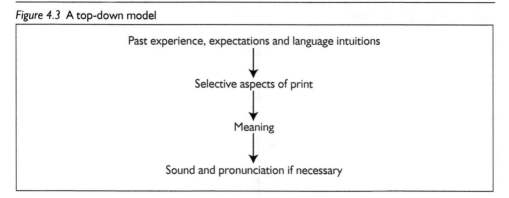

These models emphasise the meaning rather than the code of reading. They assume that the learner learns to read by gradually picking up the parallels between reading and listening. So the reader does not need to develop any conscious knowledge of the features of written language; however, this may later lead to a heavy reliance on memory.

Other models of reading include the apprenticeship approach which links learning to read and learning to speak. Learners listen to a teacher reading while they follow the text in a book and then attempt to read along until they feel able to 'read' some or the entire book by themselves (Waterland 1988). The basic ideas of this approach are derived from Goodman's 'psycholinguistic' approach to reading (1970). Interactive models of reading see reading as a perceptual and a cognitive process, in which the reader uses both previous experience and the 'code' features of the text to create meaning. This model underpins the National Literacy Strategy model of reading development. The range of strategies can be depicted as a series of searchlights, each of which sheds light on the text. Successful readers use as many of these strategies as possible:

- phonic (sound and spelling)
- knowledge of context
- grammatical knowledge
- word recognition and graphic knowledge

The Ofsted report *The National Literacy Strategy: The First Four Years 1998–2002* criticised the searchlights model on the grounds that it 'gave insufficient emphasis in the early stages to the teaching of phonics' (Ofsted 2002: 3).

The alphabetic principle is the key to a productive writing system; an infinite number of words can be produced from a small, reusable set of letters. Learners must develop a basic appreciation of the alphabet principle; they must develop a deep and ready knowledge of spellings and spelling-sound correspondences; the capacity to read with fluency; and reflective comprehension (Adams 1990). Alphabetic systems can be problematic. English has multiple derivatives from other languages and pronunciation irregularities. Learners taught phonic models of reading learn the sounds that the letters of the alphabet usually make, so that they can work out words for themselves. Learners should be able to 'sound' out any new words they come across. A report by HMI (1990) found 'a clear link between higher standards and systematic phonics. Phonic skills invariably formed a part of the repertoire of those who showed early success in reading'. The evidence suggests that learners taught by this approach do better in the longer term than those taught by other methods (Chall

1979; Johnson and Baumann 1984). Nevertheless, a study by Dolch and Bloomster (1937) had concluded that a mental age of seven years was necessary for a child to use phonics. Phonological codes, however, can operate at the level of rhymes (Goswami and Bryant 1990) and these can prove useful to young learners.

> In order for a child to understand something, he must construct it himself, he must reinvent it. Every time we teach a child something, we keep him from inventing it himself.
>
> (Piaget 197:27)

Guided reading and writing is the counterpart to shared reading. The essential difference is that, in guided work, the teacher focuses on the development of independent reading and writing, rather than modelling the processes for learners. Paired reading is a more structured form of shared reading with an individual child. Initially a book is chosen that the learner wants to read but before reading the general content is discussed the teacher and learner agree on a prearranged signal, such as a tap on the table, or a touch of an arm. If this is used during the session it indicates that the learner wants to take over the reading. When the learner makes an error (miscue) the teacher says the correct word, the learner repeats the word and then continues. If the learner hesitates or struggles with a word the teacher waits for about five seconds before supplying it. This continues throughout the session. Good teachers use a range of approaches to teaching reading gained through a wealth of knowledge and skills which can be drawn upon in a flexible manner according to the needs of individual children (Lee and Gupta 1995).

Writing

> The child in the classroom, just like a professional writer, needs to learn a craft, but very early on can begin to create his or her unique voice.
>
> (Hayhoe and Parker 1992:9)

Written text can be utilised as a tool for extending knowledge and understanding of ideas and experience. Writing communicates meaning in a permanent form. Meek (1991) identifies this as making thinking visible, an opportunity to express thinking. Writing is undertaken for an audience and for a function (Schools Council Programme 1972). The sense of audience is important in determining how the writing is done. In schools the main categories of audience are as follows

- learner to self
- learner to trusted adult
- learner to teacher as partner in dialogue
- learner to teacher seen as examiner or assessor
- learner to peers (as expert, co-worker, friend, etc.)
- writer to readers (unknown audience)

Writing serves different functions and can be conceptualised as a continuum. See Figure 4.4.

Figure 4.4 Writing as a continuum

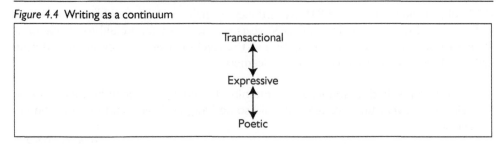

Expressive writing reflects the ebb and flow of the writer's thoughts and feelings. Transactional writing involves the presentation of facts and poetic writing is imaginative writing.

 Task 4D

Think about the writing learners carry out.
Which audiences do they write for?
What functions of writing do they engage in?

An audience matters in writing. If the audience is the teacher who will mark the writing then marking matters (Benton 1981). Thus audience and function can be seen as forces acting upon writing. The national literacy strategy has incorporated these into the teaching objectives and extended the range of writing to include genre, the characteristics that the writing takes stressing the link between writing and reading and indicating that the two activities reinforce each other. The context of pupils' reading, i.e. the texts, gives structure, themes and purposes for much of their writing, while the focussed teaching of word and sentence level skills contributes to the organisation and accuracy of their writing. The form in which the teacher gives marks or makes comments on the learners' scripts can also have cumulative effects beyond those probably intended and it is important to think about what is being made rewarding.

Binns (1978) theorised that learners must first be motivated to write and then need the opportunity to talk, listen and formulate ideas. Reflection on the task is a key element before any writing is committed to paper. Preliminary notes need to be made culminating in a first draft, which is subsequently edited. A final copy that is proofread signals the end of the process. Parker (1993) outlines a writing process with more detailed stages. This is conceptualised in Figure 4.5.

Using story to develop reading and writing

> An oral story can be told and retold, and each time it can be changed, embellished, elaborated or simplified. Story telling is a dramatic improvisation, a symbolism, where speakers and listeners construct and occupy worlds of their own creation. Through voice and eye and gesture, the listener is drawn into a story, woven into the tale as a participant, to feel anger, fear, despair, and joy. Story telling is interactive: it moves the listener back and forth from spectator to participant. The storyteller achieves this through inflection, emphasis, cadence, pace, pause and register.
>
> (Corden 2000: 147)

Figure 4.5 The writing process

Pre-writing stage   1.　　　Context   2.　　　Preparation   3.　　　Models   4.　　　Planning
Drafting stage   5.　　　Samples   6.　　　Conferencing   7.　　　Drafting   8.　　　Redrafting   9.　　　Proofreading
Post-writing stage   10.　　　Publication   11.　　　Review   12.　　　Reflection

Story is a medium by which every learner can enter into language. Fictional worlds offer a chance to reflect on the actual without being entirely bound by it. Stories are a way of seeing things through the eyes of others and in this way we can broaden our perceptions of the world. It stimulates the imagination by creating new people and places in your mind. Anticipation and retrospection encourage predictive skills as learners follow the pattern of events to formulate endings. The act of listening to a story can enhance learning. Story telling and listening prompt not just the development of literacy but the thinking that underlies it. In addition, listening to and telling stories focuses the learner's attention on aspects of spoken language such as language diversity, change and consistency in language, the differences between oral and written versions of the same story; the structures and conventions of oral narrative and enable us to develop personal storytelling skills (Howe and Johnson 1992:8).

Rosen (1998) suggests that it is through writing that we celebrate and record the variety and richness of oral language. He argues that writing:

> … can record playground songs, stories my granddad told me, a tongue twister my friend told me, funny things our dads say when they stand in front of the mirror. It can represent dialect, monologue, dialogue, jokes, commands, pleadings, intimate chats, and gossip. Much of this is a highly undervalued, uncherished area of human creativity. It exists as a main carrier of our culture and identity, and yet children in schools get few chances to record it and celebrate it. Writing it does give them that possibility.
>
> (Rosen 1998: 23)

Shared writing provides many opportunities to learn, apply and reinforce skills in the context of a larger group with careful guidance from the teacher. Teachers should use texts to provide ideas and structures for the writing and in collaboration with the class, compose texts, teaching how they are planned and how ideas are sequenced and clarified and structured. Shared writing is also used to teach grammar and spelling skills, to demonstrate features of layout and presentation and to focus on editing and refining work. It should also be used as a starting point for subsequent independent writing. Guided writing sessions should be used to teach pupils to write independently. The work will normally be linked to reading, and will often flow from work in the whole class shared writing session. These sessions should also be used to meet specific objectives and focus on specific aspects of the writing process, rather than on the completion of a single piece of work.

Assessing reading and writing

Reading can be assessed in a variety of ways. Graded reading tests provide a 'reading age', which may or may not be the same as a learner's chronological age. These are standardised tests and words assessed are not taken in context. Results, therefore, may not reflect the true capabilities of the learner. A miscue analysis (Goodman, 1978) is based upon the theory that the mistakes a learner makes when reading aloud from a text betray a great deal about how they are tackling the reading task. A reading conference/interview is time consuming but can offer a quality evaluation of a learner's progress in reading (Holdaway 1980). Other classroom activities, which provide opportunities for assessment of reading comprehension, include whole group and small group discussion, creative responses (writing from a different character's point of view), drawings (of descriptive passages), active approaches to text (choosing favourite lines), dramatic presentations and representing texts in different media (narrative to drama; poem to newspaper article). A reading journal is a simple note of the book, page and response to the reading, which can be completed, by the teacher or teaching assistant.

Similarly, we can use a range of methods to assess writing. A graded writing assessment that works in the same way as a graded reading test can give an indication of whether the learner is functioning within the accepted norms for their age. Using response partners, where learners assess each other's writing and talk about it afterwards can promote developmental dialogue. A writing conference, a focussed writing discussion that addresses targets that have been set can be a way of establishing ownership of the process of writing development. It is clear that tasks involving reading and writing are interlinked and thus assessment strategies have to be clear in order to establish the skill being measured.

Drama

The action of drama as a form of literacy should not go unnoticed. Through drama we can provide experiences that contribute towards meaningful models of language development and learning. Drama offers contexts for learning, which could not normally be part of an everyday classroom environment. Drama can transport learners into an alternative narrative that they might not otherwise experience. Drama can provide a way of exploring the multiple literacies, which are not part of the traditional curricula, for example looking at community languages, topics such as gender, multicultural and health education.

Barriers to communication

Acquiring a language and becoming literate are not necessarily automatic. Barriers can exist which inhibit the development of language and literacy skills. Where a learner has difficulties in language and literacy there are implications for learning across the curriculum. There may be language or semantic problems where words and symbols may mean different things to different people. Also disorganised ideas and the use of the wrong word or phrase may lead to poorly expressed messages, which confuse rather than enlighten. We may be affected by our own beliefs and values in a way that predisposes us to listen to and interpret some messages more accurately than others and which may present particular difficulties for interpersonal relations (Riches 1994). It is also possible to exercise control and power through the choice of what information is imparted or withheld. Or we may simply choose an ineffective form of communication.

For some learners there are specific communication problems that can prevent effective communication. These problems can be identified as primary or secondary, the former being specific speech or language impairment (developmental dysphasia), and the latter, a communication problem as a result of a medical condition or intellectual impairment. In some instances it may be difficult to distinguish between the two and where learners display challenging behaviour it may not be clear whether this is the cause or the effect of the speech and language difficulty (Wintgens 1996). We will now look at some of these difficulties in a little more detail.

Expressive problems may affect the form and content of what learners have to say. Word order or grammatical structures may be used inappropriately. Some learners may not have the physical ability to produce sounds accurately or the voluntary control to produce sounds at will (dysarthria and dyspraxia). In some cases learners may use alternative or augmentation communication systems (ACC) – such as a signing system (Makaton; Paget Gorman Signed Speech) or a symbol system (Rebus; Makaton Symbols; Blissymbolics) to supplement speech. Pragmatic problems can mean a difficulty in interacting and are closely linked with social behaviour. How to initiate or end a conversation or how to take turns when talking will prove harder. Learners may have difficulties with non-verbal communication so that they have poor eye contact, use gestures inappropriately or fail to appreciate culturally acceptable distances, which people maintain when conversing with others. Receptive problems are less obvious to identify as they relate to comprehension and understanding. These can also be overlooked due to the prominent nature of expressive language difficulties Wright (1995). Those in this category will interpret instructions literally and have difficulty with sarcasm and verbal humour. Abstract concepts will be alien and making inferences and predictions difficult. A lack of understanding of the relationship between cause and effect may create potentially dangerous situations for them where they are unable to predict consequences of actions. Despite their lack of comprehension, such children often have expressive language. Learners who echo the teacher's words or those of others or whose own conversation is plentiful, yet meaningless, may have this problem.

The SEN (Special Educational Needs) Code of Practice (2001) refers to 'communication and interaction' needs that may be diverse and complex. Moreover, learners can manifest these difficulties consistently over time, in particular settings or parts of the curriculum. The range of difficulties covered by this definition includes those identified above as well as those with specific learning difficulties (SpLD) such as dyslexia. Learners with visual and hearing impairments fall within this definition as do learners who demonstrate features within the autistic spectrum – including Asperger's Syndrome. Learners within this group may be described as having moderate, severe or profound learning difficulties (MLD, SLD, and PMLD). People working with learners who have speech and language difficulties should be able to make observations that reflect knowledge and understanding of the processes of communication and language within the overall development of the learner. They should be able to recognise the nature of communication and language difficulties and their effects on learning and be able to plan, implement and evaluate intervention for learners. In

Figure 4.6 The effect of modelling upon performance

The elements not present in modelling are:	*While the elements present are:*
Competition;	Cooperation;
Exclusion;	Acceptance;
Criticism;	Approval;
Coercion	Invitation to join in.

addition they should be able to reflect on their own spoken and written communication skills (Wright 1995).

Strategies for supporting language and learning

Corden (2000) identifies ways in which we can support learning in language and literacy by:

 Modelling: showing children examples of work produced by experts.

 Demonstrating: illustrating the procedures experts go through in producing work.

 Supporting: giving aid to children as they learn and practise procedures.

Modelling is a powerful way of supporting literacy development. Holdaway (1979) highlighted the 'corporate experience' of shared reading as a powerful mode of learning. Holdaway argued that teachers model strategies and stimulate independent and small group reading and writing activities through a shared examination of texts. Modelling is most effective when the learner feels able to succeed and perceives that the task is purposeful. They need to be confident enough to take risks and to respect and trust the teacher. Figure 4. 6 outlines the effect of modelling upon performance.

Demonstrations can teach learners about aspects of what readers and writers have to do. Each demonstration shows an aspect of the power of written language. Demonstrations provide opportunities for learners to engage in the purpose of the activity, to share their intentions with the demonstrator, whether to construct a story or to discover what someone else is thinking or planning. They are not formal decontextualised instructions (Smith 1984). Teachers can be explicit about the purpose of reading and writing as well as about the conventions of how meanings are communicated or transferred to and from the page.

We can support the development of literacy through scaffolding. Bereiter and Scardamalia (1987) affirm the notion of 'reflective activity' in successful writers. Teachers need to help learners develop a greater degree of conscious awareness of their thought processes while reading and writing. Explicit awareness raising and instructional practice should be an essential ingredient of literacy teaching where children are exposed to a range of good literary models and made explicitly aware of the composing process. They need to participate in focussed discussion of texts and develop process-writing strategies. They also need to be able to reflect on their own knowledge and strategies and evaluate their own progress.

Adult literacy

The adult core curriculum for literacy provides a map of the range of skills and capabilities that adults are expected to need in order to function and progress at work and in society. Research by the Basic Skills Agency has identified three attainment groups that make up the seven million adults in the United Kingdom with problems in literacy and/or numeracy. There is a group who need fairly modest help to 'brush up' their skills to the required level; a group who have greater difficulty and need more specific and in-depth help; a group who require intensive teaching by specialist teachers. In addition, there is a group for whom English is an additional language. A specific curriculum has been developed for this group of learners.

The adult literacy core curriculum shares the basic principles of inclusion and access that are set out in the National Curriculum for schools. Education is identified as:

> a route to equality of opportunity for all, a healthy and just democracy, a productive economy, and sustainable development. Education should reflect the enduring values that contribute to these ends. The curriculum secures ... for all, irrespective of social background, culture, race, gender, differences in ability and disabilities, an entitlement to a number of areas of learning and to develop knowledge, understanding, skills and attitudes necessary for their self-fulfilment and development as active and responsible citizens.
>
> (DfES 1999)

Literacy and ICT

Word-processing is the ultimate new literacy. Meek (1991) reveals that computers help us to learn about learning and about language and other symbol systems, their nature and functions. She argues that the focus should not be on the machine, but what we think we are doing with it. As a literacy tool, a computer depends on who is in charge. Word processing has made pupils less afraid of making spelling mistakes and of getting going in writing. Many learners are better motivated to work on tasks that include information and communication technology (ICT). Computers give us more information and more choice about what we do with it, different ways of communicating and changing what we want to say. It is important to note that there is an increasing emphasis on the use of ICT from adult to adult, via fax and e-mail and through internet facilities. As a consequence it is well to remember that as we increase the forms of literacy we may likewise increase the forms of illiteracy and exclusion. The Language Master is an efficient and manageable way of enabling less able learners to be independent with supplementary reading resources for a range of schemes, as well as for separate phonic and word recognition skills.

A literate environment

It is important to create in the workplace an environment that is rich in natural and functional language, and encourages learners to be part of that creative process,. We need to incorporate this environment into the three key areas of work, play and living (Goodman and Goodman 1979). The acknowledgement of all of a learner's literacies and those of their cultures and communities is also a vital part of the process, building outwards to develop their experiences into wider realms.

> The school and the family share the responsibility of preparing the young person living in a world of powerful images, words and sounds. Children and adults need to be literate in all three of these symbolic systems, and this will require some

assessment of educational priorities. Such reassessment might well result in an integrated approach to the teaching of language and communication.

(UNESCO 1982)

Summary

In this chapter we have explored the role of language in learning and the ways in which we learn language skills. We have considered the importance of talk for learning and other types of communication strategy. The function and importance of speaking and listening, reading and writing and the impact they have on developing learning have been outlined. We have looked at the barriers that can delay language acquisition and the ways in which learners can be supported. In turn we hope that this has re-enforced the importance of all forms of literacy and given you some food for thought. The following documents will provide you with more detailed information if you would like to follow up any of the issues raised.

  Bibliography

Abercrombie, K. (1968) 'Paralanguage', *British Journal of Communication*, 3, 55–9

Adams, M. (1990) *Beginning to Read* (A Bradford Book), Cambridge, MA: The MIT Press.

Argyle, M. (1983) *The Psychology of Interpersonal Behaviour*, Harmondworth: Penguin.

Argyle, M. (1988) *Bodily Communication*, 2nd edn, London: Routledge.

Assessment of Performance Unit (APU) (1988) *Surveys of Language Performance: Assessment Matters*, London: Department of Education and Science.

Atkinson, M. (1992) *Children's Syntax: An Introduction to Principles and Parameters Theory*, Oxford: Blackwell.

Baddeley, G. (ed.) (1992) *Together Through talk KS1 and 2*, Sevenoaks: Hodder and Stoughton.

Barnes, D. (1976) *From Communication to Curriculum*, Haromondsworth: Penguin.

Barnes, D. (1992) 'The role of talk in learning', in Norman, K. (ed.) *Thinking Voices: The Work of the National Oracy Project*, London: Hodder and Stoughton.

Bates, E., Camaioni, L. and Volterra, V. (1975) 'The acquisition of performatives prior to speech', *Merrill-Palmer Quarterly*, 21, 205–26.

Benton, A. (1981) 'Aphasia: historical perspectives', in Sanron, M.T. (ed.) *Acquired Aphasia*, New York: Academic Press.

Bereiter, C. and Scardamalia, M. (1987) *The Psychology of Written Composition*, Hillsdale, NJ: Lawrence Erlbaum.

Binns, R (1978) *From Speech to Writing: A Teacher Technique for Use with Slow Learners*, Edinburgh: Scottish Curriculum Development Service

Bruner, J.S. (1966) *Towards a Theory of Instruction*, Cambridge, MA: Harvard University Press.

Bruner, J.S. (1971) *The Relevance of Education*, London: Allen and Unwin.

Bruner, J.S. (1975) 'The ontogenesis of speech act', *Journal of Child Language*, 2, 1–21.

Bruner, J.S. (1976) 'Learning to do things with words', in Bruner, J.S. and Garton, A. (eds) *Human Growth and Development*, Oxford: Oxford University Press.

Bruner, J.S. (1986) *Actual Minds, Possible Worlds*, Cambridge, MA: Harvard University Press.

Chambers, A. (1991) *The Reading Environment*, Gloucester: Thimble Press.

Chall, J. (1979) 'The Great Debate: ten years later, with a modest proposal for reading stages' in Resnick, L.B. and Weaver, P.A. (eds) *Theory and Practice in Early Reading*, Vol 1, Hillsdale, NJ: Erlbaum Associates.

Chomsky, C. (1979) 'Approaching reading through invented spelling', In Resnick, L.B. and Weaver, P.A. (eds), *Theory and Practice of Early Reading*, Vol 2, Hillsdale, NJ: Erlbaum Associates.

Corden, R. (2000) *Literacy and Learning through Talk*, Buckingham: Open University Press.

DeLunga, G.A. (1927) *Speech: Its Function and Development*, New Haven, CT: Yale University Press.

DES (1990) *The Teaching and Learning of Reading in Primary Schools: A Report by HMI*, London: HMSO.

DfES (1999) *The School Curriculum and the National Curriculum: Values, Aims and Purposes*, London: HMSO.

DfES (2001) *Special Educational Needs Cone of Practice*, London: HMSO.

DfES NLS (1997) *Framework for Teaching Literacy*, London: HMSO.

DfES NNS (1997) *Framework for Teaching Numeracy*, London: HMSO.

Dolch, E.W and Bloomster, M. (1937) 'Phonic readiness', *Elementary School Journal*, XXXVIII (November, 1937), 201–5.

Frith, U. (1985) 'Beneath the surface of developmental dyslexia' in Patterson, K., Coltheart, M. and Marshall, J. (eds) *Surface Dyslexia*, Hove: Erlbaum.

Goodman, K.S. (1970) 'Reading: a psycholinguistic guessing game' in Singer, H and Ruddell, R.B. (eds) *Theoretical Models and Processes of Reading*, Newark, DE: International Reading Association.

Goodman, K.S. and Goodman, Y.M. (1979) 'Learning to read is natural', in Resnick, L.B. and Weaver P.A. (eds) *Theory and Practice of Early Reading*, Vol 1, Hillsdale, NJ: Erlbaum Associates.

Goodman, Y. (1978) 'Kid-watching: an alternative to testing', *Journal of National Elementary Principals*, 57(4), 41–5.

Goodwin, P. (1999) *The Literate Classroom*, London: David Fulton Publishers.

Goswami, U. and Bryant, P.E. (1990) *Phonological Skills and Learning to Read*, Hove: Erlbaum.

Hall, E.T. (1966) *The Hidden Dimension*, New York: Doubleday.

Hayhoe, M. and Parker, S. (eds) (1992) *Reassessing Language and Literacy*, Buckingham: Open University Press.

HMI (1990) *The Teaching and Learning of Reading in Primary Schools*, London: HMSO.

Johnson, D.D. and Baumann, J.F. (1984) 'Word identification' in Pearson, P.D. (ed.) *Handbook of Reading Research*, London: Longman.

Holdaway, D. (1979) *The Foundations of Literacy*, Sydney: Ashton Scholastic.

Holdaway, D. (1980) *Independence in Reading*, London: Ashton Scholastic.

Howe, A. and Johnson, J. (1992) *Common Bonds: Storytelling in the Classroom*, London: Hodder and Stoughton.

Johnson, D. and Bauman, J. (1984) 'Word identification' in Pearson, P.D. (ed.) *Handbook of Reading Research*, New York and London: Longman.

Johnson, D. and Johnson, R.(1990) 'What is co-operative learning?', in Brubacher, M., Payne, R. and Rickett, K. (eds) *Perspectives on Small Group Learning: Theory and Practice*, Ontario: Rubicon.

Lee, V. and Gupta, P. (eds) (1995) *Children's Cognitive and Language Development*, Buckingham: The Open University Press.

Lewis, M. and Wray, D. (1998) *Writing Across the Curriculum: Frames to Support Learning*, Reading: Reading and Language Information Centre, The University of Reading.

Light, P. and Glachan, M. (1985) 'Facilitation of individual problem solving through peer interaction', *Educational Psychology*, 5(3–4), 217–25.

Meek, M. (1991) *On Being Literate*, London: Bodley Head.

Mercer, N. (1995) *The Guided Construction of Knowledge: Talk amongst Teachers and Learners*, Clevedon, OH: Multilingual Matters.

Molloy, J.T. (1979) *Dress for Success*, New York: Wyden.

Neill, S. and Caswell, C. (1993) *Body Language for Competent Teachers*, London: Routledge

Ofsted (2002) *Annual Report of Her Majesty's Chief Inspector of Schools: Standards and Quality in Education 2002/03*, London: The Stationery Office.

Parker, S. (1993) *The Craft of Writing*, London: Paul Chapman Publishing.

Piaget, J. (1954) *The Construction of Reality in the Child*, New York: Basic Books.

Piaget, J. (1972) *The Psychology of the Child*, New York: Basic Books.

Riches, C. (1994) 'The hidden therapy of a prison art education programme', in Liebmann, M. (ed.) *Art Therapy with Offenders*, London: Jessica Kingsley Publishers.

Riches, C. (1997) 'Communication in educational management', in Crawford, M., Kydd, L. and Riches, C. (eds) *Leadership and Teams in Educational Management*, Buckingham: Open University Press.

Rosen, M. (1998) *Did I Hear you Write?* 2nd edn, Nottingham: André Deutsch.

Schools Council Programme (1972) *Language at Work*, Schools Council Programme in Linguistics and English Teaching Papers: Series II, Vol 1, London: Longman.

Smith, F. (1984) 'The creative achievement of literacy', in Goelman, H., Oberg., A. and Smith, F. (eds) *Awakening to Literacy*, Portsmouth, NH: Heinemann Educational Press.

Sutton, C. (1981) *Communicating in the Classroom*, London: Hodder and Stoughton.

UNESCO (1982) *Declaration on Media Education* Paris: UNESCO.

Vygotsky, L.S. (1965). *Thought and Language*, Cambridge, MA: MIT Press.

Vygotsky, L.S. (1978) *Mind in Society*, Cambridge, MA: Harvard University Press.

Waterland, L. (1988) *Read with Me: An Apprenticeship Approach to Reading*, Stroud: Thimble Press.

Wells, G. (1987) *Language and Learning at Home and at School*, London: Hodder and Stoughton.

Wells, G. (1986) *The Meaning Makers: Children Learning Language and Using Language to Learn*, Portsmouth, NH: Heinemann Educational.

Wells, G. (1989) 'Language in the classroom: literacy and collaborative talk', *Language and Education*, 3(4), 251–74.

Wilkinson, A., Davies, A. and Berrill, D. (1990) *Spoken English Illuminated*, Buckingham: Open University Press.

Wintgens, A. (1996) *Links between Emotional Behaviour Problems and Communication Difficulties*, London: David Fulton Publishers.

Wood, D. (1991) 'How children learn', in Light, P., Sheldon, S. and Woodhead, M. (eds) *Learning to Think*, London: Routledge

Wray, D. and Medwell, J. (1991) *Literacy and Language in the Primary Years*, London: Routledge

Wright, J.A. (1995) 'Provision for children with communication difficulties', in Lunt, I., Norwich, B., Wright, J. and Kersner, M. (1998) *Supporting Children With Communication Problems: Sharing the Workload*, London: David Fulton Publishers.

Chapter 5

Numeracy

This chapter is divided into four main sections: The Developing Curriculum; The National Numeracy Strategy; Assessment; and Supporting Mathematics. Thus we will provide you with a brief history of the mathematics curriculum and the important events that have led to establishing what is taught in the classroom today. We cover the need for using practical equipment within the Daily Numeracy Lesson. We will then explore the integration of ICT to augment current teaching methods. Opportunities for developing mathematical skills and learning experiences outside the classroom are also discussed.

The developing curriculum

The fundamental elements of the mathematics curriculum have remained relatively unchanged over the past 100 years. The 'Revised Code of 1862', which primarily introduced 'the three R's' (reading, writing and arithmetic) into schooling, has links with objectives in the current National Numeracy Strategy (NNS) (Brown 1999). What has been changed, however, is the impetus on mathematical understanding, teaching and delivery techniques. We will now develop a picture of the changes that have happened within the mathematics curriculum.

Understanding versus ignorance

> There has been a tension between accurate use of calculating procedures and the possession of the 'number-sense' which underlies the ability to apply such procedure sensibly.
>
> (Brown 1999: 3)

In other words, whilst learners can be taught the procedures of mathematics, they need in addition a sense of its application to problems in life outside the educational setting. An illustration of this problem could be one where a learner has successfully learned their seven times table but their ability to apply this knowledge in a practical sense is limited. If the learner is later employed in a theatre and then has to work out the best way of distributing a coachload of fifty-seven theatre goers around an auditorium with seven seats in each row, the question becomes can they do this easily applying the mathematical understandings developed earlier? This tension between the technical application of mathematical principles and a deeper understanding of them has been a major contributor to the changes that have been witnessed in the teaching of mathematics (Brown, 1999). The basics of mathematics, the four rules, shape recognition, and so forth have always been part of written and unwritten curricula and underpin the objectives within the Numeracy Framework. What has changed is the importance of learners' understanding of mathematics, rather than just being able to solve calculations. Brown refers to this as having 'number sense'.

The Cockroft Report: *Mathematics Counts* (1982) attempted to address such issues. Although the committee investigations and reports were based mainly on practice in secondary schools, the report has had an impact on primary education and on the teaching of mathematics in general. The Report produced many recommendations. Two which have had a significant impact on the current curriculum are the inclusion of practical applications and the inclusion of using practical resources and equipment. This has led to the use of exploration and play in mathematics (Merttens, 1996; Brown, 1999). 'The emphasis shifted from facts to be learned to problems to be solved' (Merttens, 1996: 45).

Why was there a need for these changes? Prior to the Cockroft Report the Nuffield Mathematics Project (1964–71) was having an impact on the ways in which mathematics was taught in schools. The Project aimed to incorporate investigation and a practical focus to mathematics teaching. Influenced by the Plowden Report (1967) and the then current trends of the Piagettian 'child centred learning' movement, the Nuffield Project created a set of pupil booklets. These resulted in children working from their own 'tailored' books and consequently there was a dramatic decline in the direct teaching of mathematics reported (Merttens 1996).

Teaching and delivery techniques

The delivery of mathematics has certainly changed, especially over the past ten years. The Cockroft Report (1982) identified the need for changes in the teaching of mathematics to incorporate more exploration, discovery learning and problem solving although this did not imply a return to the practice seen in the 1960s of 'no teaching'. Local Education Authority Numeracy Consultants were employed to support teachers in this process. The current curriculum reflects the present emphasis on teaching. Directed teaching, as discussed further in the chapter, is now specifically written into the National Numeracy Strategy (NNS), and can be clearly seen in the Unit Plans created for teachers. This has resulted in an increased directed and interactive teaching so that learners are now more involved in the learning process. Games, practical resources and questioning techniques, all augmented by ICT resources are features of mathematics teaching. Figure 5.1 shows featured 'highlights' of development in the mathematics curriculum.

Figure 5.1 provides you with a brief outline of the key developments that have impacted on the mathematics curriculum. It is worth remembering that changes in mathematics education are linked to the politics, economics and culture of the time in which they are developed. Currently organisations are noticing the impact of inclusion. Whilst this has not directly changed the mathematics curriculum it has altered the organisation of mathematics education, with teachers and TAs meeting the needs of a very diverse range of learners. Additionally, there are changes in education theory that impact upon practice. We have

Figure 5.1 The development of the mathematics curriculum

The Revised Code of 1862	Formalising the Three R's into schools (reading, writing and arithmetic).
1955 *The Teaching of Mathematics in Primary Schools*: A Report by the Mathematical Association	The beginnings of adopting a child-centred approach.
Nuffield Mathematics Project (1964–1971)	The project incorporated investigation and mathematical understanding. Some problems with pupil workbook approach.
Mathematics 5–11: A Handbook of Suggestions (DES 1979)	To steer the contents of the primary curriculum.
The Cockroft Report 1982	First commissioned in 1977 by a Labour government, to investigate the teaching of mathematics in schools.
Primary Initiatives in Mathematical Education (PrIME) 1985	Headed by Hilary Shuard, mostly known as the Calculator Aware Number Curriculum Project (CAN), putting in effect of the sensible use of calculators in primary schools.
Task Group on Assessment and Testing 1987	
The Education Reform Act 1988	The introduction of the National Curriculum for all subjects, including revisions in 1991, 1995 and Launch of Curriculum 2000.
The introduction of National Testing 1996	SAT's introduced.
The introduction of the National Numeracy Strategy 1997–1998	NNS introduced into schools, massively impacting on planning, assessing and teaching.
Introduction of Unit Plans 2001–2002	Unit Plans – pre-written plans for teachers to annotate and modify. Published by the DFES

already indicated that there was a Piagettian influence on the curriculum. It remains to be seen how much of an impact 'Mind-friendly' learning techniques such as the impact of 'Mind Mapping' will have on mathematics education, particularly in the recording of mathematics.

The National Numeracy Strategy

The National Numeracy Strategy (NNS) created a framework for the delivery of numeracy within schools. First introduced into schools in 1997–8 it came with a wealth of support materials. The framework, not to be confused with the National Curriculum, can be seen as a guide or vehicle for delivering the objectives set by the National Curriculum. If a school was particularly strong in the teaching of mathematics it may see the framework as constraining and therefore choose not to follow it; however, this has proved unusual .The impact of the introduction of the NNS cannot be underestimated. It influenced all aspects of the mathematics curriculum including the planning, objectives, assessment, delivery of teaching and school support. In fact it even altered the title of the subject. In primary schools today the term 'numeracy' is used more widely than the term mathematics.

So, what is numeracy? To find a clear definition is difficult. Many will argue that it describes the building blocks of mathematics. It is not, as many believe, only concerned with number. The framework also includes 'shape and space' and other mathematical concepts. At its simplest we can define numeracy as encompassing all mathematics below GCSE standard. Hence the more complex concepts, e.g. trigonometry, are not involved. Mathematics can also be seen as a language, with numeracy providing the beginnings or building blocks of that language. We can't ask learners to speak fluently until they have learned the basics in any language. Nevertheless the key aim of the NNS is ultimately about raising standards. Famously David Blunkett (Secretary of Education 1997–2001) was confident enough to bet his job on it. So how was the strategy able to raise standards? Two initiatives, which were central to the Framework's objectives, were the increase in mental strategies to solve calculations and directed, interactive whole-class teaching. These will be discussed further in the chapter.

The framework introduced a new format for planning in schools, both short- and long-term. Each year group has its own set of objectives which can be split into five 'strands':

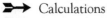 Number and the number system
 Calculations
 Solving problems
 Measure, shape and space
 Handling data

A sixth strand – Algebra – is included in the Years 7–9 Framework. For each year group there is a prescribed set of objectives – approximately 100 per year group. The Framework sets out when these objectives should be taught/met in schools. For example in Year 2 'Counting and properties of number' will be taught for the first three days of the Autumn Term, then revisited at specific times throughout the year. This highlights one of the underpinning concepts of the strategy, namely the carefully planned teaching sequence that sees topics/ideas being targeted for a specific number of days and then returned to later in the year. This replaced the former method whereby teachers would teach a topic such as 'time' for X weeks until the majority of the class had 'got it'. The framework is designed to give shorter, sharper bursts of concentration on a topic. Obviously, this may not be suitable for all children and not all practitioners agree with this method.

Not only did the NNS introduce a new way of planning but a new Daily Mathematics Lesson (DML) was introduced. This was a three-part lesson which was intended to have a brisk pace. An outline can be seen in Figure 5.2.

Figure 5.2 clearly shows how the Strategy has changed the nature of the day-to-day teaching of mathematics. It also shows the inclusion of the mental and oral starters at the very beginning of every DML. This 'starter' does not have to be linked to the main body/objectives of the lesson; however, it must be explicitly teaching or revising a mental strategy for the children to use. Many think of this 'starter' as a warm-up similar in many respects to the warm-up an athlete may complete prior to a training session. Instead of informing the body that a training session is imminent and preventing later injury, the oral and mental 'starter' informs the learner's brain to 'switch' to a more logical thought process. Mental and oral starters are exercises that encourage learners to be able to carry out and solve problems in their heads. This is not to imply that they were not present prior to the strategy; however, the NNS has formalised them. To see how this works consider a learner in Year 3 being asked to add 46 + 45 in their head. The framework provides examples of how calculations should be addressed both mentally and formally (written). The learner

Figure 5.2 Outline of a Daily Mathematics Lesson

	Whole class/ groups/ individual	Examples of what these individuals might be doing within the Daily Mathematics Lesson		
		Teacher	Learner	TA
Mental and oral starter 5–10 mins	Whole class	Rehearsing, sharpening and developing mental and oral strategies, e.g. using games – mathematical Noughts and Crosses.	Working with whole class, being interactive with teaching.	Supporting individual or group. Repeating questions, giving further explanations.
Main teaching activity 30–40 mins	Whole class/ groups/ individual	Teaching input and pupil activities.	Working on set activity. Could be individual or in groups. Recording in books/computer.	Supporting individual or group. Working with group, playing a number game or reinforce teaching of concept.
Plenary 10–15 mins	Whole class	Summarising key facts of lesson, addressing misconceptions etc.	Working with whole class. Explaining how they have completed their work, what they have learnt.	Supporting individual or group. Leading group in explaining work to the class.

should recognise that 46 + 45 is double 45 plus 1. Strategies such as this are built upon over time as the learner experiences the Framework. Although teachers are always expected to use their professional judgment and therefore allow learners to solve problems in the best way for themselves, problems can occur when learners use such strategies during homework activities. In addition, parents may not understand the strategy and certainly not the 'bigger picture' of building up the child's skills at the correct pace.

An omission from Figure 5.2 is the inclusion of whole-class interactive teaching. Figure 5.3 shows how this might be incorporated into the DML.

Figure 5.3 Inclusion of whole-class interactive teaching in the Daily Mathematics Lesson

	Whole Class/ Groups/ Individual	Examples of what these individuals might be doing within the Daily Mathematics Lesson		
		Teacher	Learner	TA
Directed teaching 10–15mins	Whole Class	Interactive teaching of a mathematical concept or problem. Use of questioning techniques, sharing ideas, use of ICT.	Engaged in the interactive teaching.	Supporting a group in this part of the session. Giving praise to those answering correctly, providing hints to those struggling, being a role model.

This part of the lesson would fall at the beginning of the 'Main Teaching Activity' as shown in Figure 5.2. The direct teaching aspect of the NNS clearly addresses the problems seen in the past of little teaching taking place. Current trends in ICT resources, including interactive teaching programmes, commissioned by the Strategy and private software companies, coupled with the more affordable hardware such as interactive whiteboards, interactive voting systems and tablet laptops are making directed teaching more accessible to practitioners.

Unit Plans

Units Plans, first piloted in 2001–2, are available for use in every school's numeracy planning. Unit Plans are weekly planning sheets, which have been pre-written by the DfES and are designed for teachers to copy/download and modify according to the needs of their own classroom and learners. For example, teachers may annotate the plans to show where they are using a certain computer program or a group is using a textbook. What is interesting about the Unit Plans is that they include planning for 'Teaching Activities' – what the teacher will be teaching during the lesson.

Vocabulary

To emphasise the importance of the mathematical vocabulary to be used within schools, the DfES (1999) produced *The National Numeracy Strategy – Mathematical Vocabulary*. This document explains how this vocabulary must be introduced to children through a range of strategies which include questioning, listening to others, sketching and labelling. What must be recognised, especially in the early years, is that the development of mathematical language must be planned for and that the correct usage of a mathematics vocabulary is vitally important in the child's understanding of the subject. Misconceptions can lie in both the mathematical understanding of a concept and in the actual understanding of a term. A common mistake would be the intermixing of ratio and proportion.

 Task 5A

Can you explain the difference between ratio and proportion?
Do you know which year group are introduced to these terms?

Proportion and ratio are introduced to learners in Year 4 and Year 5 respectively. They are difficult concepts to explain so don't worry if you got it wrong! These are the definitions:

> Ratio – part-to-part comparison, irrespective of the whole. For example – 'there are three red cubes for every four blue cubes' the information given does not include the total number of cubes. This ratio would be expressed as 3:4 red to blue cubes.

> Proportion – Part to whole comparison. For example – 'three out of four cubes are red, hence three quarters of the cubes are red'. Proportion can be given as a fraction, percentage or decimal notation.

This is just one example of how the misuse of terms can cause confusion for learners. It also demonstrates how as professionals we must keep abreast of terms and vocabulary. Having the correct definitions to hand is always a good technique, even with young children.

Task 5B

Can you define the following terms and know in which Year group they are first introduced?
Venn diagram
Pictogram
Vertices
Translation
Congruent
Estimate

All TAs involved with numeracy should ensure that they have their own personal copies of the mathematics vocabulary booklet and that they are familiar with the terminology they will be using with learners.

Assessment

Assessment within numeracy will incorporate all of the major forms of assessment. Three of those forms are explained in more detail: formative, summative and diagnostic assessment.

Formative assessment (also referred to as assessment for learning) is the assessment completed on the day-to-day basis. This assessment is mostly informal and ongoing. Examples would include notes made by teachers on learners' records, learner discussions, ongoing assessment records, grades and comments in learners' books. In the numeracy lesson this would be seen in the assessments made by a teacher, possibly at the end of a week on a set of objectives. Current mathematics software can now be used in a formative fashion. The key to all of these assessments is that they ascertain the level a learner has reached and should also inform how the future planning can be adapted to maximise learning.

Summative assessment (also referred to as assessment of learning) can be seen as the formal aspect of assessment. The most commonly recognised assessment to fall into this category would be the end of Key Stage SATs tests and GCSEs. Assessments such as SATs are obviously given enormous recognition by schools and their stakeholders. However what must be recognised is that assessments such as these are a 'snapshot' assessment of a learner. They do not provide a more detailed picture built up over time like formative assessment.

Diagnostic assessment is of particular importance in mathematics. An example of diagnostic assessment in mathematics would be the analysing of a learner's work to identify misconceptions within a calculation. This assessment would not only identify where a learner is having difficulties but also identify the problem of understanding itself. For example if a teacher were to mark the following questions in a summative fashion the questions would be marked as incorrect. When marked in a diagnostic fashion, the teacher can identify what misconceptions the child has.

Example 1	Example 2	Example 3	Example 4
23	23	36	36
+28	+28	−28	−28
41	411	12	18

Task 5C

Prior to reading the next paragraphs, can you diagnose the misconceptions made in each of the examples?

In Example 1 the learner has added the digits together without carrying into the tens column. Example 2 shows that the learner is carrying the ten created by adding the 3 and 8. However, instead of adding that to the 2 and 2 in the tens column they have inserted this into the tens column, relegating the 2+2 = 4 into the hundreds column. This not only shows that the learner has a misconception of the carrying process but also in place value and in not identifying that the answer given (411) is obviously too large. The learner is relying too much on number fact, rather than 'number sense'. Example 3 shows that the learner has not completed subtraction by decomposition and has taken away the smaller digit in the column from the larger one. Example 4 indicates that decomposition has taken place however the 3 in the tens column has not been replaced with a 2 in the process.

Task 5D

Faced with learners presenting these misconceptions, how would you address these problems?

Addressing misconceptions is a large part of mathematical teaching. Look at Diagram 5.1.

Diagram 5.1 Boxes

The two boxes above look identical. Most of us will assume that the larger box is heavier. However, understanding the concept that the smaller box may be filled with stones and the larger box with feathers, making the small box heavier, is a conception that some learners may find hard to understand. Demonstrating and teaching this concept can be very challenging, when the learner finds the idea hard to perceive. Faced with problems such as these, practical resources are used to enable experience to enhance mathematical understanding.

The same frustrations can be said about teaching the concept of time which can be problematic for some learners. The topic of time has several elements which include:

➤ measuring lengths of time
➤ converting between measurements of time
➤ the concept of times of the day
➤ analogue clocks
➤ 24 hour clock.

If we think about the number skills needed to tell the time accurately we can see how learners make mistakes. We use a decimal system, hence the largest number that can be put into a unit, ten or hundred, indeed into any column is 9. Once the number is larger the digit returns to 0 and the digit in the next column to the left rises by 1. If we think about the 12-hour clock, minutes can go up to 60 and only then do they return to 0. Even more confusingly, hours make their way up to 12 and then return to 1. By understanding the misconceptions we can really teach the child what they need to know.

Special Educational Needs Coordinators (SENCOs) should make staff aware of such misconceptions. Figure 5.4 is adapted from the SENCO's Training Pack, part of the NNS support material.

Supporting mathematics

The SEN Code of Practice (2001) suggested that implementation of support be introduced in a 'graduated response'. Within the NNS and the National Literacy Strategy this was a process known as Wave Intervention. Wave Intervention is split into three sections. It encompasses all learners and sees support moving from quality teaching for all through to specific one-to-one support. In 'Wave One' the effective inclusion of all in a high-quality daily mathematics lesson is assumed. This is known as 'quality first teaching'. Additionally, within schools, learners may be at any point on the normal graduated response of the

Figure 5.4 Ways of resolving misconceptions

Year	Objective	Preparatory activities	Misconception	Teaching
6	Read and plot co-ordinates in all four quadrants.	Recognise negative whole numbers in context.	Think that -6 is larger than -2 because 6 is larger than 2.	Give children experience of counting back into negative numbers so that they hear the pattern in the numbers. Count on and back into negative numbers on a counting stick – in a vertical and horizontal orientation.

will have more success with numeracy as a subject. Even with older children there can be an identifiable effect on attainment. A 'number-rich environment' at home will involve children in mathematical terms and ideas, such as:

➤➤ Asking how long a TV programme is on for.
➤➤ Using money to buy sweets and calculating change .
➤➤ Singing counting songs, – for example 'One, Two, Buckle My Shoe'.
➤➤ Sorting and resorting the washing into colour piles or object piles.
➤➤ Cooking using measurements of mass and heat.

These tasks have been conducted in families for many years and so may seem very obvious. However, when carrying out such activities the adult in charge must remember the mathematics involved and concentrate upon the development of language and mathematical concepts. These learning opportunities need to be introduced and supported by the school. Parents need assistance and guidance to support their children. Many may feel inadequate and under-confident about their own mathematical skills and therefore doubt their ability to support their child's mathematical progress. Others may not have the time. Other problems can occur with parents not understanding the processes that children are required to carry out in order to complete a calculation or solve a problem. Earlier in the chapter it was discussed how the NNS Framework builds children's understanding up over the years. This can mean that parents, who have been taught in a different way, may confuse a child when intervening (Fraser and Honeyford 2000). However, these pitfalls should not deter us from the fact that home and the wider learning environment have a massive impact on children's learning and must be addressed when planning for learning.

Summary

The importance of mathematics within our daily lives cannot be underestimated. With ever-changing technologies impacting upon our daily lives in an increasing number of ways, many of the skills needed to access and use these products are based on aspects of mathematical thinking. Without a good grounding in mathematics learners are likely to find themselves at a distinct disadvantage compared with their peers. TAs must be aware of the learner's capabilities and desired outcomes in order to support them to reach their potential. A lack of understanding of the curriculum objectives, mathematical concepts, support strategies and the way that the learner best acquires mathematical understanding will lead to the learner failing to receive effective support.

Conclusion

In this chapter we have looked at the development of mathematics and the National Numeracy Strategy in schools and considered the importance of developing mathematical concepts. We have shown that concepts of maths can be taught through practical example and have stressed the need to be able to convert the technical ability to answer mathematical problems to solving problems in the wider world. We have also looked at the ways in which understanding of mathematics can be supported. If you would like to find out more then look at the following section for pointers to further reading.

📖 Bibliography

Brown, M. (1999) 'Swings of the pendulum in numeracy: issues past and present', in Thompson, I. (ed) *Issues in Teaching Numeracy in Primary Schools*, Buckingham: Open University Press.

Central Advisory Council for Education (1967) *Children and their Primary Schools* (The Plowden Report), London: HMSO.

DES (1988) The Education Reform Act, London: HMSO.

DES (1982) *Mathematics Counts* (The Cockcroft Report), London: HMSO.

DfEE (1999) *The National Numeracy Strategy, Framework for Teaching Mathematics from Reception to Year 6*, London: Cambridge University Press/HMSO.

DfEE (2001) *Springboard 4: Catch up Programme for Children in Y4*, London: DfEE.

DfES (2001a) *The National Numeracy Strategy, The Daily Mathematics Lesson: Guidance to Support pupils with Dyslexia and Dyscalculia*, London: DfES.

DfES (2001b) *The Special Educational Needs Code of Practice* London: HMSO.

DfES (2002) *The National Literacy and Numeracy Strategies, Including All Children in the Literacy Hour and Daily Mathematics Lesson: Summary of Provision for Children with Special Educational Needs*, London: DfES.

Fraser, H. and Honeyford, G. (2000) *Children, Parents and Teachers Enjoying Numeracy: Numeracy Hour Success Through Collaboration*, London: David Fulton.

HMI (1979) *Mathematics 5–11*, London: HMSO.

Mathematical Association (1955) *The Teaching of Mathematics in Primary Schools*, London: Bell.

Merttens, R. (ed.) (1996) *Teaching Numeracy*, Leamington Spa: Scholastic.

National Curriculum Council (1985) *Calculators, Children and Mathematics* (The Report of the Calculator Aware Number Curriculum Project), London: Simon & Schuster.

Nuffield Foundation (1964) *Nuffield Mathematics Project*, London: W.R. Chambers & Murray.

Chapter 6

Science

> The great achievement of the sciences, over the past three or four hundred years, has been to tell us important and interesting things about ourselves and the world in which we live... it presents the world in novel and surprising guises, saying that things are in reality often not what they seem to be ...Acting on the reliable knowledge which science has produced, scientists have developed a staggering variety of artefacts and products, ranging from electric motors to antibiotics, and from artificial satellites to genetically engineered insulin for treating diabetes, which have transformed our lives and lifestyles as compared with those of past generations.
>
> (Millar and Osborne 1998: S4.1)

In this chapter we introduce ways of thinking about science and the theories of learning development that have been influential in relation to the Science curriculum. We explore the nature and organisation of the science curriculum and provide a brief historical account of the development of it. The impact of language in science and the importance of developing learners' use of terminology are discussed and suggestions are made throughout about ways in which adults can support scientific development. We also look at the importance of particular Health and Safety considerations that are related to science. Finally, we discuss the potential of ICT in science education and the inter-relationship between science and design technology is explored.

The development of the science curriculum

In the early 1960s influential reviews of the aims and objectives of the science curriculum were published (Ministry of Education 1962; Association for Science Education 1961). What followed was a major curriculum initiative in science, which led to the development of the Nuffield Science Project. The aim of the Nuffield project was to 'assist teachers to help children through discovery methods to gain experience and understanding of the environment and to develop their powers of thinking effectively about it' (Harlen 1975: 2). A review of curriculum projects produced as a result of the Nuffield initiatives revealed that practical work tended to be designed to get the 'right' answer whereas true experimentation was only rarely present (Association for Science Education 1961). During this review and development period the Assessment and Performance Unit (APU) was set up by the DfES in 1974 in response to a perceived need to find out what was happening in schools in key areas of the curriculum. The APU science project monitored pupil performance in schools and its findings had a powerful impact upon the development of the science curriculum. The APU view stressed the need for and importance of the personal investigative nature of science and that scientific knowledge and understanding had to be demonstrated within and outside school across different contexts. The school science curriculum review (SSCR) (1985) also found this investigative emphasis lacking and stated that schools were taking a view of science as a cultural activity where knowledge is constructed rather than discovered.

> In their early experiences of the world, children develop ideas, which enable them to make sense of things that happen around them. A child brings these informal ideas to the classroom … the aim of science education is to adapt or modify these original ideas to give them more explanatory power. The ideas of young children … tend to be limited to concrete observable features … As they get older their ideas become adapted to fit with a wider range of experiences and evidence.
>
> (DES 1988: Para 2.9–2.10)

In other words, children learn through experiences, through trial and error, through building and testing, through their use of language. Learners actively construct an interpretation of the world using these experiences compared with and set against existing knowledge. As their learning progresses so does the sophistication of the challenges they set themselves. This corresponds to the process scientists use to construct knowledge. Science education therefore should seek to build upon learners' existing ideas to give them explanatory power by providing them with the ability to think, act and talk scientifically. Woolnough and Allsopp (1985) in their critique of the role of practical work noted that science had two distinct elements. First, there is the knowledge base which involves the content and concepts that science holds up as important. Second, there is a set of processes which the scientist uses to investigate.

Scientific concepts are generalisations that have been developed in order to group particular events or objects together based on similarities between them. For example if we think about a table, this is a concept that we recognise. When we see a new table we instantly recognise it because of its generalisable features – a flat surface and four legs. When faced with something new we make judgements about what this might be by testing it with our existing knowledge or concepts. We can then build upon the concepts that we already have or indeed be introduced to new concepts. Scientific processes are what we use when we want to make sense of the information in the world around us or want to discover something knew. Scientists use them to advance knowledge about how and why things work. Learners use them to make sense of the events and their observations as they engage with their expanding experiences. These processes are used interactively. Examples of process skills include the ability to observe, ask questions, identify problems, suggest explanations, make predictions, design investigations and experiments, prepare and use apparatus, measure, make decisions based on evidence, communicate findings and apply knowledge to new situations. Processing skills need to be systematically taught and opportunities to enhance and develop them incorporated into science education.

There is a distinction to be made between the processes we have just explored and scientific procedures. Procedures need to be taught. It is the procedures that set out what

Figure 6.1 Interaction within conceptual understanding

we need to do to investigate particular phenomena. The procedural knowledge learners gain enables them to identify what is relevant in an investigation or experiment and allow them to collect reliable data. A procedure is a specific way of doing science which the scientific community refines over time. Content, processes and procedures all interact with each other within the learner's existing conceptual understanding of the phenomena they encounter. This can be represented by Figure 6.1.

Distinguishing content, process and procedures in science education enables us to assess learning more effectively. For example, if a primary-school-aged child is trying to investigate which material is the most effective for making a waterproof tent and they test material using different amounts of water we don't assume that this means that they have no concepts of materials or their properties (Concepts) or that they are having difficulty in selecting the most appropriate ways of investigating and exploring the phenomena (Processes). It may be that they lack knowledge of the necessity for a fair test (Procedures). This is the aspect of their scientific learning that needs to be developed. A critical part of the APU review was to develop an assessment framework to represent learners' scientific achievement defining the appropriate activities, contexts and content. The materials created by the APU defined and exemplified many aspects of science education that had previously been ignored through setting practical tasks.

Whilst this approach to learning is based within 'constructivist' thinking (learners construct their own meanings through experiencing) Shayer and Adey (1981) used Piagettian stages of development to analyse the demands of the Nuffield science curriculum. Piaget theorised that children's thinking was different from adults' and that the child needed to progress through four developmental stages each growing out of the one preceding it. These stages consist of a complete organisation of concepts, strategies and assumptions which represent a different way of thinking about the world. Piaget did not think that the environment shaped the child, but rather the child actively seeks to understand his environment. Piaget concluded, from his experiences with IQ testing, that children's minds were organised differently to those of adults. He began to think that what distinguished children's thought from adults was not the sheer amount of knowledge, but the complexity of type of thought. It was this that inspired him to research the mental structures (referred to later as schemas) of children as they grow. Figure 6.2 outlines Piaget's conceptualisation of the schemas.

Figure 6.2 Piaget's conceptualisation of schemas

Stage	Age	Nature of schemas	Description
Sensorimotor	0–2 yrs	Practical action	Initially the child will make sense of the world through their reflexes, sensory perceptions and physical actions upon objects and the world allowing them to develop a 'practical' or 'sensorimotor' knowledge of objects in time and space.
Pre-operational	2–6/7 yrs	Symbolic (but not logical)	The child realises that actions can be performed upon objects, but that they don't have to take place in reality they can be performed 'in the head', perhaps using imagery. An understanding of symbols and what they represent in reallife develops.
Concrete-operational	6/7 –11 yrs	Logical and mathematical	The child has the ability to reason about the world of objects, time, number, space and causality. They can deal with two or more aspects of a situation at the same time.
Formal-operational	11 yrs +	Logical and mathematical abstractions	The concluding stage occurs during adolescence. The adolescent is able to think in a logical fashion, is able to hypothesise, test and revise in the light of the results. This may occur practically or mentally, but it is an indication that they have achieved the end state of human cognition.

The Cognitive Acceleration through Science Education (CASE) project is also based on Piagettian ideas. Shayer and Adey (1981) identified a gap between the demands of a course and the learner's cognitive levels. They suggested that different types of science teaching could influence the rate at which cognitive power develops as practices and learning needed to be set to an appropriate stage for the learner to develop, which would then encourage the learner to move on to the next stage. Shayer and Adey created an intervention programme designed to accelerate pupils' cognitive development during KS3 to prepare them for learning in KS4. They produced a series of activities designed to stimulate the cognitive development of pupils. The aim was to use the context of science-related activities to develop pupils' thinking skills. In the context of secondary science education, the most significant development is from the 'concrete' stage to the 'formal thinking' stage. At the concrete-operational stage the ability to be able to cope with a limited number of variables and an ability to describe but not to explain situations is a feature. During the *formal-operational stage* learners have the capability to cope with multi-variable problems and to provide explanations for events. CASE carried out research into the cognitive abilities of learners in Key Stage 3. The results of large-scale testing of pupils' cognitive abilities indicated that only 28 per cent of 14-year-olds were able to demonstrate evidence of the *formal-operational stage* and many learners never reached this stage. The science National Curriculum requires elements of the *formal-operational stage* at Level 5 and above. This can be achieved through careful lesson planning and support.

Piaget's stages of development are based on children failing certain tasks at certain ages, which led him to believe that they do not possess the required mental structure at that stage. Piaget considered formal, logical and abstract reasoning to be the culmination of human development. In order to teach effectively however we have to take account of what learners already believe and the ways in which they are making sense of their world. Margaret Donaldson (1978) argued that the context of the tasks can make the difference between a child being able to answer or not, and that children are very capable of logical thought earlier than Piaget suggests. Her arguments are centred on the fact that most reasoning is embedded both in a particular context and also in knowledge we already have. So learners go through:

> definite stages of brain growth, physical growth and development of sensory learning…. Piaget's worst legacy is in the education systems using his theories to justify not exposing young children to experiences when their senses are ideally developed to benefit.
>
> (Dryden and Vos 1997:111)

In other words, we should not be frightened to expose learners to new thinking and ideas simply because some theorists claim they are not at a stage where they are ready for this yet. Learners can surprise us with the sophistication of their ability to learn.

To summarise this section we can say that the science curriculum is based upon a constructivist perspective about learning. Learners construct a mental model of their environment and any new learning is interpreted in relation to this. They need the opportunity to manipulate objects and ideas to make sense of the world around them. Learners are not passive receivers of information; they actively engage with their environment. Science learning requires collaboration in the development of understanding. It involves a worldwide community of scientists and others in developing more powerful ways to gain an understanding the natural world. The role of adults in an educational setting is to enable the construction of meaning. Vygotsky (1978) recognised the importance of adults as mediators of new knowledge. 'Human learning presupposes a specific social nature and a process by which children grow into the intellectual life around them.' He stressed the importance of social interaction in development. A learner's ability is not merely what they can do now, but what they could do with help. The learner is seen as having a 'zone of proximal development'; a range of skills and abilities, which are accessible with assistance. This theme was developed by Bruner (1986) who saw that adults needed to 'scaffold' learning to enable progress beyond the current level of unassisted performance.

Learning depends on the knowledge, purposes and motivation that the learner brings to the task. We need to identify existing knowledge in science and plan activities which develop understanding and provide opportunities for support that take account of individual differences between learners. Constructing meaning is a continual process in which new experiences allow learners to reconsider and restructure their understanding. Scientists are also engaged in this process. As a result, scientific knowledge and explanations may change as new evidence is collected and thinking is challenged. It also follows that science does not always explain every phenomenon and whilst it may be used to solve problems it can be limited. There is also a whole area you may wish to consider about the ethical and moral dilemmas posed by scientific experiments. For example, the issues of cloning is one of the current 'big news' dilemmas faced by the scientific community.

Science in the curriculum

The 1988 Education Reform Act laid out the foundations for the National Curriculum (NC), in which science became a compulsory core subject for all pupils aged 5–16. Subsequently, there have been three major revisions to the science orders – in 1991, 1995 and 2000. Science, like the other NC subjects, has a programme of study (PoS) for Key Stages 1 to 4. The PoS is part of the statutory order, which means that it must be taught to all pupils. It sets out the knowledge, skills and understanding that pupils should learn during each key stage. The PoS for science is split into four sections. Sc1 Scientific enquiry sets out the role of ideas and evidence in science and the investigative skills that children should develop, together with the knowledge and understanding set out in:

Sc2 Life processes and living things;
Sc3 Materials and their properties;
Sc4 Physical processes.

In KS3 and KS4 PoS, Sc1: Scientific enquiry is in two parts.

Section 1.1 - ideas and evidence in science;
Section 1.2 - investigative skills.

The PoS does not say when any particular content should be taught and it is not a Scheme of Work. The Department for Education and Skills (DfES) and the Qualifications and Curriculum Authority (QCA) have developed non-statutory Schemes of Work that schools use to develop the curriculum content. Attainment Targets (ATs) set out the levels to which learners of different abilities should have developed knowledge, skills and understanding by the end of each key stage. Each AT relates to a section of the Programme of Study and is graded into eight levels that give a description of what a learner should know and be able to do.

The Key Stage 3 National Strategy is part of the Government's commitment to raising standards in schools. The Strategy was launched in September 2001 with a focus on English and Mathematics. The science strand of the Key Stage 3 National Strategy was introduced in 2002. The Framework for teaching science: Years 7, 8 and 9 is similar to the Frameworks for English and mathematics. It provides practical suggestions and advice on meeting the National Curriculum requirements for science. There are also non-statutory Schemes of Work, which schools use to develop the curriculum content.

There is a separate curriculum for the Foundation Stage – Curriculum guidance for the Foundation Stage (2000), in which science is part of the area of learning 'knowledge and understanding of the world'. This provides a structure within which teachers plan learning experiences, which lead towards the early learning goals. These goals are broken down into Stepping Stones at three broad levels, indicating progression from age three to the end of the Foundation Stage. The Foundation Stage refers to children aged three to five. Not all children, however, attend a school or nursery and at the end of the Reception Year some children may have had less than a year of formal education, whilst others might have had two years. Consequently, there are wide variations in experiences and abilities. At KS4 the programme of study is the template for GCSE qualifications. Each awarding body produces GCSE specifications that are required to conform to the NC.

Science can be organised in many ways. It may be an integral ongoing part of a theme or topic. It may be linked to another subject, such as Design Technology. The most common way of organising science is through discrete science sessions. However science is organised, it is important to make any science topic relevant by:

- using real-life starting points which are familiar to learners
- introducing items that stimulate interest
- posing a problem to be solved
- using the outdoor environment
- using simulations
- making educational visits
- inviting a guest speakers into science lessons
- using ICT

Task 6A

Think about how science is organised in your workplace.
What are the benefits and disadvantages of the way in which science is taught?

Science and Language

Talk plays a fundamental role in organising our understanding of the world. Vygotsky (1965) argued that language structures and directs the processes of thinking. Barnes (1976) saw that it was essential for learners to re-express what they know in talk in order to come fully to terms with it. Wells (1987) described how young learners used talk to 'make meaning' of their experiences.

> Engaging with others in collaborative action and in the co-construction of meaning... because this process.. involves the active transformation of the information provided by the other participant(s) in the activity, the learner's resulting knowledge is never a straightforward copy, but a new, personal, reconstruction.
>
> (Wells 1987)

A precise use of terminology is important in science to prevent learners from developing misconceptions. If we use the term 'disappear' to describe what happens when sugar dissolves in water we may be suggesting or confirming a misconception that the dissolved sugar no longer exists.

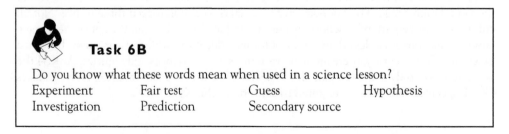

Task 6B

Do you know what these words mean when used in a science lesson?

Experiment	Fair test	Guess	Hypothesis
Investigation	Prediction	Secondary source	

Accurate vocabulary should be introduced as soon as learners enter the Foundation Stage. Each unit of a Scheme of Work for Key Stages 1 and 2: Science (QCA) has a list of scientific vocabulary to be taught, and indicates words that might cause confusion because their everyday or 'other subject' meaning differ from their scientific meanings. The words in task 6B all have a precise meanings in science. How many did you explain correctly? Look at Figure 6.3 for the answers!

Learning in science is connected with other subjects in the curriculum, for two main reasons. Firstly, developing learners' skills in other areas will result in them being in a better position to learn concepts in science. Secondly, every subject area has a responsibility to contribute to the development of core skills, in particular information and communication technology (ICT), mathematics and English. Learners can also develop thinking skills through science, described in the National Curriculum (1988) as: information-processing skills, reasoning skills, enquiry skills, creative thinking skills and evaluation skills. Written communication is also a vital tool for the development of scientific knowledge enabling learners to develop their knowledge and understanding of science. The development of literacy skills can be a means of improving pupils' scientific understanding by encouraging learners to write for a range of purposes and for different audiences. Learners need the ability to keep records and make notes when they undertake science activities. They need to be taught how to collect, record and present information in different forms. It is essential that learners can communicate their findings orally as well as in writing.

Questioning

Questions form the basis of learning in science. We use questions throughout the curriculum. 'We learn by asking questions. We learn better by asking better questions. We learn more by having opportunities to ask more questions. '(Morgan and Saxton 1991)

Morgan and Saxton identify 6 different types of questions that stimulate thinking;

➤ Questions which draw upon knowledge (Remembering)
➤ Questions which test comprehension (Understanding)
➤ Questions which require application (Solving)
➤ Questions which encourage analysis (Reasoning)
➤ Questions which invite synthesis (Creating)
➤ Questions which promote evaluation (Judging)

Figure 6.3 Scientific vocabulary

Experiment:	A controlled test to see if there is any evidence to support a hypothesis
Fair test:	A test in which variables are controlled in order to reduce any doubts about explanations of the results of the test.
Guess:	Speculation about the result of an experiment or investigation
Hypothesis:	A tentative idea or explanation to be tested.
Investigation	Looking for evidence to support an explanation or idea.
Prediction:	A forecast of what will happen, based on prior knowledge.
Secondary source:	The results of someone else's investigation or experiment, information in a book or other source (not from first-hand experimentation or investigation).

For questioning to be effective we need to choose questions that encourage learners to investigate themselves, encourage learners to use these types of questions and limit their use of the type of questions that simply require an answer to be provided. If an investigation is feasible we can help learners turn their 'Why?' questions into 'what if...?', 'What can you find out about...?', 'What happens when...?' or 'Is there a way to...?' There are two types of questions – open and closed. A closed question can usually be answered fairly quickly, e.g. 'Where did you find the earthworm?' They can be used effectively to draw attention to important points or summarise findings from a group. An open question requires more thought and encourages various responses that may act as a stimulus for further investigation, e.g. why do you think we found more earthworms in the compost than in the grass?' Open questions are effective when learners are discussing hypotheses, explaining the results of an investigation and drawing conclusions

The Children's Learning in Science (CLIS) project highlighted the issue that many learners have 'naïve' ideas that they bring with them into the classroom. They drew attention to some of these misconceptions that children (and adults) develop for the phenomena they observe. Usually these misconceptions occur because the learner has developed a common-sense explanation, for example the water that appears on the outside of a cold can of drink has come through the sides of the can. Understanding the logic behind these explanations can help us address them. The learner who thinks that water has seeped out of a can needs to learn that there is water in the air that condenses when hitting a cold surface (perhaps by observing the steam from a kettle against a piece of glass).

This notion about learners having pre-conceived ideas was incorporated into an approach to teaching that started from the premise that teaching must begin from the current ideas of the learner rather than trying to treat them as 'empty vessels'. Driver *et al.* (1994) makes an analogy to giving road directions over the phone where your first question should be 'where are you now?' (Driver *et al.* 1994: 42). The first step in this teaching approach gives learners the opportunity to make their own ideas explicit and to listen to the ideas of others. This is referred to as elicitation. Only by articulating their own ideas will they be in a position to change their understanding in response to teaching. Other stages involve exposing learners to the scientific view and providing opportunities for them to apply their existing knowledge.

Safety in science

All staff have a duty to contribute to the maintenance of a safe and secure learning environment and to minimise risk. All workplaces have policies and procedures outlining the roles and responsibilities each person has in relation to health and safety. In science you need to be aware of the potential health and safety issues. Health and Safety is governed by the Health and Safety at Work Act 1974. This states that you have a duty to:

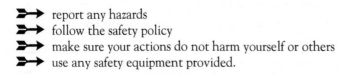

- report any hazards
- follow the safety policy
- make sure your actions do not harm yourself or others
- use any safety equipment provided.

Task 6C

Think about the hazards and Health and Safety issues that may arise in relation to science.

You need to be aware of the potential dangers that surround learners particularly in science lessons such as faulty equipment and apparatus, hygiene and health hazards, trailing electrical wires, overloaded plugs, and things that can be tripped over. As science involves exploration of the physical world there are also external hazards, such as the inappropriate use of equipment outside of a laboratory, poisonous plants, risks from animals and faeces, and risks from contaminated water in ponds and puddles. Potential risk can be avoided by common-sense precautions. Before undertaking practical work of any kind you must be sure that you can do so safely. If you are at all unsure, do not go ahead and discuss your concerns with a member of staff. Many schools conduct risk assessments for science activities (both demonstrations and class practical lessons) and have advice available for staff. Adults need to be aware of safety aspects in lessons and should provide a role model for learners with regard to safety. They should also be aware of the procedures for managing accidents and emergencies. Each workplace will have a health and safety policy that you need to make yourself familiar with.

Using ICT

ICT can be used to support science teaching in many ways. Making use of computers to assist with practical work (data logging) is probably the most important ICT application in science. Sensors can monitor physical quantities such as temperature and pH and the data can then be passed to a data logger being presented on a computer screen. Computer simulations can extend what is possible via hands-on practical work to include activities, which would be difficult, dangerous or time-consuming to conduct in reality. Access to large sources of data on CD-ROMs or via the internet can be used to support learners.

Science and design technology

Science and design technology are closely related subjects. The overlap between the two subjects is most noticeable when a using a technology task to demonstrate a scientific principle: for example, making a moving toy to develop learners' understanding of how the different joints in the body operate. There is a clear distinction to be made, however, between learning which helps us to understand and explain how the world operates and learning which is directed towards understanding a single artefact (a toy), system (manufacturing) or environment (a kitchen as a workspace). This latter is covered in the design technology curriculum. The integration of science and design technology can be valuable when we want learners to see an application for scientific concepts within a technological solution.

Summary

As humans we develop meanings and understandings of the world around us by actively exploring, investigating and discussing it with others. The curriculum for science is based upon a social constructivist interpretation of learning. The role of the teacher is to bridge the gap between what the learner already understands about the world, what others know about the world and what can be demonstrated through experiment. The social context of science should make us aware that science is a cultural activity with implications for the world around us. Consequently the inter-relationship between Science and other curriculum subjects is important. We can develop literacy, numeracy and ICT skills through science education and there is a close link between Science and Design Technology that is mutually supportive. Scientific language helps learners to construct knowledge of the world and is very important in developing their understanding of scientific concepts. The correct use of scientific language is important in helping learners to solve their misconceptions about science.

 Task 6D

Reflect on the ideas raised in this chapter about the nature of learning in science.
How does this correspond to your own personal experience of learning science?
How can you use what you have learned to support the scientific development of learners in your context?

Conclusion

This chapter has provided you with a basic introduction to some of the key ideas underpinning science education. Science is constantly developing and keeping up-to-date with information is important for all those who support learning in science. We have demonstrated that the science curriculum can be understood in terms of the content, the processes and the procedures that learners will cover. The processes required to engage with science, however, are applicable across other subjects even though the procedures used may be closely linked to the scientific community. We can support scientific learning through the careful use of language and by using questions to elicit current levels of understanding. We can then provide tasks that will enable the learner to move from existing knowledge to new knowledge about the phenomena they experience. For more information related to sciences the following list may be of some help.

Bibliography

Adey, M,, Shayer, P., and Yates, C. (2001) *Thinking Science* (3rd edn), Cheltenham: Nelson Thornes.

Association for Science Education (ASE) (1961) *School Science Review*, Hatfield: Association for Science Education.

Association for Science Education (ASE) (2001) *Be Safe!* (3rd edn), Hatfield: Association for Science Education.

Barnes, D. (1976) *From Communication to Curriculum*, Harmondsworth: Penguin.

Brook, A., Briggs, H. and Bell, B. (1983) 'CLIS (Children Learning In Science) summary report: aspects of secondary students' understanding of particles', in *Secondary Students' Ideas about Particles*, Leeds: Centre for Studies in Science and Mathematics Education, The University of Leeds.

Bruner J.S. (1971) *The Relevance of Education*, London: Allen and Unwin.

Bruner J.S. (1986) *Actual Minds, Possible Worlds*, Cambridge, MA: Harvard University Press.

DES (1988a) *Science for Ages 5 to 16*, London: HMSO.

DES (1988b) *Task Group on Assessment and Testing*, London: Department of Education and Science.

DfEE (1988) *Science: A Scheme of Work for Key Stage 3*, London: DfEE.

DfEE (1998) *Science: A Scheme of Work for Key Stages 1 and 2*, London: DfEE.

DfEE (1999) *The National Curriculum Handbook for Primary Teachers in England*, London: DfEE.

DfES (2000) *Curriculum Guidance for the Foundation Stage*, London: DfES.

Donaldson, M. (1978) *Children's Minds*, London: Fontana.

Driver, R., Squires, A., Rushworth, P. and Wood-Robinson, V. (1994) 'CLIS (Children Learning in Science)' *Making Sense of Secondary Science Research into Children's Ideas*, London: Routledge.

Dryden, G. and Vos, J. (1997) *The Learning Revolution*, Auckland: The Learning Web.

Education Reform Act 1988.

Harlen, W. (1975) *Science 5/13: A Formative Evaluation*, London: Macmillan Education/Schools Council.

Health and Safety at Work Act 1974.

Millar, R. and Osborne, J. (1998) *Science Beyond 2000: A Report with 10 Recommendations*, London: King's College.

Ministry of Education (1962) *Statistics of Education: Part I: 1961* London; HMSO.

Morgan, N. and Saxton, J. (1991) *Teaching, Questioning and Learning*, London: Routledge.

School Science Curriculum Review (1985) *Science Education for a Multicultural Society*, Leicester: SSCR/Leicestershire Education Authority.

Vygotsky, L.S. (1965) *Thought and Language*, Cambridge, MA: MIT Press.

Vygotsky, L.S. (1978) *Mind in Society: The Development of Higher Psychological Processes*, Cambridge, MA: Harvard University Press.

Wells, G. (1987) *Language and Learning at Home and at School*, London: Hodder and Stoughton.

Woolnough, B. (ed.) (1991) *Practical Science: The Role and Reality of Practical Work in School Science*, Buckingham: Open University Press.

Woolnough, B. and Allsopp, T. (1985) *Practical Work in Science*, Cambridge: Cambridge University Press.

Chapter 7

Information and communication technology (ICT)

Information and communication technology (ICT) plays a major part in the curriculum. The application of ICT is included as a statutory requirement of the core subjects. It is also included in the Foundation Stage curriculum and as a Key Skill in Post-Compulsory education. In this chapter we will explore why we should teach ICT and look at the current curriculum requirements for it. We will go on to consider the various ways in which the teaching and learning of ICT can be delivered within schools and the implications for good practice. We will also address the management and organisation of ICT.

What is ICT?

The following definition is taken from the guidance in the QCA Schemes of Work for ICT:

Information and communications technologies (ICT) are the computing and communications facilities and features that variously support teaching, learning and a range of activities in education.

Examples of ICT activities can include the use of:

- broadcast material or CD-ROM as sources of information;
- micro-computers with appropriate keyboards and other devices for literacy and writing;
- keyboards, effects and sequencers in music teaching;
- devices to facilitate communication for pupils with special needs;
- electronic toys to develop spatial awareness and psychomotor control;
- e-mail to support collaborative writing and sharing of resources;
- video-conferencing to support the teaching of modern foreign languages;
- internet-based research to support geographical enquiry;
- integrated learning systems (ILS) to teach basic numeracy;
- communications technology to exchange administrative and assessment data.

The National Curriculum focuses on the practical applications of ICT. This means that learners should be able to understand how information is structured in a database, possess the ability to search the internet, use computers to construct simulations, be able to use a range of common software products e.g. word processing or e-mail to communicate effectively. Learners should understand that ICT can be used for managing and controlling processes. In addition, they should have knowledge of how to use ICT securely and have an awareness of ethical considerations such as the right to privacy and ownership of material. The particular focus of ICT is on learners' capability with ICT. This is why Information Technology (IT) is the overall title used for the National Curriculum subject and qualifications. Not all IT learning involves the use of computers.

Task 7A

Think about the teaching of IT in your workplace.
What methods, other than the use of computers, are used to deliver the IT National Curriculum?

You my have recorded some of the following:

➤➤ Sorting physical objects to introduce databases
➤➤ Using a highlighter pen to mark key words in a text that could be used in an electronic search
➤➤ Learners taking it in turns to give each other directional instructions as part of teaching in control systems

Why should we teach ICT?

Using computers to assist learning is not a recent development. The advent of computer technology in the 1970s was accompanied by a growth in software applications aimed at the education marketplace. Many of these early computer programs were used to reinforce particular aspects of learning. Skinner (1938–1989) believed that learning occurred when a particular behaviour is reinforced and that immediate reinforcement was the most beneficial. This was referred to as 'programming learning' and early computer programs adopted this model. These types of programs were heavily criticised, however, by people such as Seymour Papert (1980) who was influenced by Piagettian ideas. Papert argued that using the computer should be revelatory for learners, content free and learner directed. In other words the computer was a tool that learners could use to further their own learning. Papert believed that learners would develop higher order thinking skills and 'powerful ideas' if exposed to this form of computer experience. Papert developed his own computer language which he believed would enable learners to engage fully with the process of directing the computer. This was called LOGO.

Kemmis et al. (1977) identified different 'paradigms of learning' that are helpful in explaining the ways in which ICT has been used within education. The early computer programs already mentioned fell into an 'instructional paradigm' whereas the learners who develop their knowledge and skills through discovery of the program at their own pace are

Figure 7.1 Paradigms of learning and computers

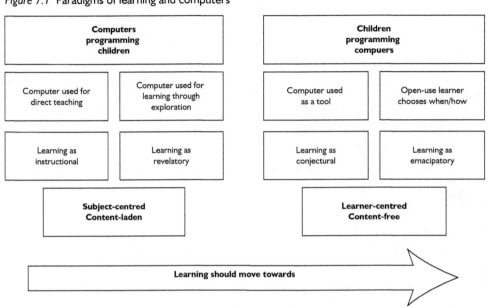

encompassed by the 'revelatory paradigm'. Within a 'conjectural paradigm' learners use a computer to test and refine their own hypotheses. It is, however, only in the 'emancipatory paradigm' when the learner begins to control the computer. The relationship between the paradigms of learning and computers is summarised in Figure 7.1.

Task 7B

Think about the reason for teaching ICT?
What arguments would you provide to someone who was sceptical of the need to deliver an ICT curriculum?

There are some critiques of the increasing emphasis on ICT within education. Beynon and Mackay (1989) have argued that technology is not and can never be apolitical or neutral. They note that people have a tendency to regard computers as unbiased and neutral which is true in relation to hardware. The software, however, is a human creation and should be open to the same level of critical interpretation as other media. Similarly, the design and content of the curriculum lies within a political, historical, economic and social structure which reflects the current perceived importance of the subject. For example, one argument for the need to teach ICT is that industry needs ICT skills. Nevertheless, if you consider the educational contexts within which ICT is taught they do not reflect those within industry. Moreover, the rapid changes in industry and their needs are not reflected in the continual change and adjustment of the ICT curriculum. There are nonetheless justifications for teaching ICT (some of which will be addressed later in the chapter). ICT is central to modern life. All of our homes have devices or systems that rely upon the computer chip. The World Wide Web (WWW) has increased access to information and the speed at which it can be obtained. Being able to use computer applications is increasingly becoming a key skill in the workplace at all levels. ICT can serve as a powerful motivator for learning and can enable the delivery of a differentiated curriculum. In addition and if used appropriately computers can develop higher-order thinking skills to extend learning beyond the instructional paradigm.

The National Curriculum

Information and communications technology (ICT) and e-learning (learning via the internet) can make a significant contribution to teaching and learning across all subjects and for learners of all ages. ICT is a tool that can provide opportunities to engage and motivate learners as well as meet individual learning needs. It can link education and home and enable educational organisations to share information and good practice. As a consequence ICT can support educational leadership and management. Since 1998 there has been a very significant investment in ICT in education. In the maintained sector this has been through the National Grid for Learning Programme (NGfL). In 1998 the NGfL Programme set out a comprehensive strategy for the development of the use of ICT provision in schools. Most schools are now connected to the internet and they have ever-increasing numbers of computers in classrooms and/or in specially designed computer suites. The intention of the NGfL programme was to improve educational outcomes through higher standards of attainment and the acquisition of important ICT skills. It was also intended to make learning more differentiated and customised to individual needs and to enable teachers to deliver an engaging, enjoyable and exciting curriculum (though it is important to note that this is dependent on the teachers' understanding of how computers can be best used to deliver such outputs).

For learners the advantage of an ICT-based curriculum is in the enhanced flexibility of study patterns that computers make available. This is particularly important in relation to the widening participation debate. Learners with special educational needs, disabilities and those unable to attend school due to illness or disaffection could all benefit from e-learning opportunities. The use of computers can increase some learners' motivation, especially if they enjoy using them, though again it is important to understand that learners need to be carefully guided in order to gain the most from such experiences. Learners can also receive personalised feedback on their progress through different forms of e-assessment. There are also advantages for parents of younger learners as ICT could provide opportunities for them to become better informed about their child's progress given the possibilities for a greater access to information and guidance relating to the education system in general, their school in particular and the school's performance. It is possible therefore to use ICT to encourage and enable parents to become more active members of the school community. In addition, with the rising importance and stress on community access to learning, schools are increasing opportunities for the community to access their ICT facilities.

The National College for School Leadership has developed an initial framework for defining e-confidence. This identifies ten key features that the e-confident school should display. These are:

➤ high levels of staff confidence, competence and leadership
➤ re-engineered teaching, learning and assessment

➤ leading and managing distributed and concurrent learning
➤ effective application within organisational and management processes
➤ coherent personal learning development, support and access – for all leaders, teaching and non-teaching staff
➤ secure, informed professional judgement
➤ appropriate resource allocation to ensure sustainable development
➤ availability, access and technical support
➤ learners with high ICT capability
➤ school as the lead community learning and information hub

Task 7C

Using the NCSL ten point checklist evaluate the e-confidence of your school.

Planning for ICT

There is one attainment target for ICT. This outlines the knowledge, skills and understanding that learners of different abilities and maturities are expected to have by the end of each key stage. There are eight level descriptions of increasing difficulty, plus a description for exceptional performance above Level 8. Each level descriptor describes the types and range of performance that learners working at that level would typically demonstrate. The level descriptors provide the basis for making judgements about learners' performance at the end of Key Stages 1, 2 and 3. At Key Stages 4 and 5, national qualifications are the main means of assessing attainment in National Curriculum subjects. The programmes of study contain two sets of requirements – Knowledge, Skills and Understanding and Breadth of Study. Within Knowledge, Skills and Understanding a number of statements are given that indicate what pupils should be taught. The Breadth of Study identifies the contexts, activities, areas of study and range of experiences through which the Knowledge, Skills and Understanding should be taught

In 1998 the DfEE and the Qualifications and Curriculum Authority (QCA) issued a Scheme of Work for Information Technology (IT) at Key Stages 1 and 2. This was subsequently updated in 2000. In the same year (2000) QCA issued a Scheme of Work for ICT at Key Stage 3. These schemes of work are non-statutory, are designed to help with planning and they also have an accompanying guide. The guides highlight links within Key Stages, across subjects and between different Key Stages within the same subject, showing ways that units can build on preceding work and how they link to other units. The guides also outline ways in which non-classroom based activities can enhance learning and develop breadth of study across the whole of the curriculum. Ways in which the units can link with and support literacy, numeracy, thinking skills and key skills are provided. This guidance and the plans form the basis of the Scheme of Work in schools. An ICT Scheme of Work should provide long and medium-term plans that show how and when learners will gain the Knowledge, Skills and Understanding outlined in the programme of study together with how this will be covered. This provides the basis from which staff will plan lessons to meet the needs of all learners. The Scheme of Work details the teaching and learning objectives and key ideas to be covered. This enables concepts to be developed systematically and also helps to plan assessment and make cross-curricular links.

At Key Stage 1, there are no statutory requirements to teach the use of ICT in the programmes of study for the non-core foundation subjects. The Curriculum Guidance for the Foundation Stage (2000) has both direct and indirect references to the use of ICT. There should be opportunities to:

➤ control a programmable toy e.g. a floor robot
➤ become aware of technology in the environment
➤ stimulate interest in ICT and other technology
➤ teach simple skills in the use of equipment e.g. switching computers on and off
➤ help children understand how things work by allowing them to take apart and reassemble equipment
➤ build on the ICT skills that children develop at home
➤ teach and encourage the use of ICT e.g. tape recorder, programmable toys, paint program
➤ provide opportunities in the role-play areas to use ICT.

It is important that adults introduce the language of ICT and become a role model encouraging young learners to observe and talk about the use of ICT. This may include encouraging them to show each other how to use ICT equipment and also provide opportunities for the use of ICT to develop skills across other areas of learning. At Key Stage 2 the Programme of Study offers progression in terms of the range of contexts within which learners should experience the use of ICT, the ICT tools that they should use and their features. The Programme of Study for Key Stage 3 extends the range of contexts within which learners use ICT, the ICT tools that they should use and the features of the tools. Learners begin to apply their skills, knowledge and understanding to solve specific problems in different contexts and are often required to make use of more than one application to complete a task. At Key Stage 4, a range of information sources and ICT tools should be used to find, analyse, interpret, evaluate and present information for a range of purposes. Skills should also be taught that include the ability to make critical and informed judgements about when and how to use ICT.

Opportunities for developing key skills are incorporated through the subject of ICT and Curriculum 2000 provides a framework for using ICT across the curriculum. Most schools have identified opportunities where ICT can contribute significantly to learning in other areas of the curriculum.

 Task 7D

How are ICT opportunities incorporated across the curriculum in your workplace?

Progression and continuity

Progression in ICT capability is concerned with the acquisition of ICT skills. But skills alone are not enough. Learners need to consolidate skills by applying them to a variety of contexts and reflecting on their use of ICT. Progression develops when learners begin to select the ICT tools they want to use. This might mean that they will select and confidently use ICT tools they are familiar with but they should also develop new skills in response to the needs of a particular task. As a result continuity in ICT capability is the responsibility of all staff and where different people have responsibility for the same learners, it is important that they work together to establish and maintain continuity.

Task 7E

How is continuity ensured in your workplace?

To achieve continuity there needs to be opportunities to discuss, agree and adopt collective approaches to planning, assessing and recording the use of IT. This should take into account resources, methods of classroom organisation and teaching and learning styles.

Organisation and management of ICT

In primary and special schools the way ICT is taught and used is usually determined by the amount and deployment of hardware. Some schools have chosen to create a computer suite whilst others have retained classroom-based ICT hardware. If a suite is used it is essential to ensure that learners are able to apply new knowledge, understanding and skills in other curriculum areas, which may not be delivered in the suite. When an ICT suite is not available, it is important to ensure that learners have opportunities to learn and practise skills, as well as to apply them. In secondary schools there are three approaches to developing ICT capability that are commonly used. Some schools teach ICT through a discrete course, some schools have embedded ICT across the curriculum and others use a combination of discrete course and cross-curricular work. Discrete courses can result in thorough coverage of ICT but appear to lack an ability to show its application to 'real life' contexts. Developing ICT skills through simply working across the curriculum can lead to learners missing some aspects of ICT or not progressing beyond basic skills. Consequently some combination of the two techniques would seem to be valuable. Whichever model of delivery is undertaken it is however important to ensure that all learners have equal opportunities to participate. During lessons learners should be encouraged to think about the activity they are engaged in and why they are doing it. They should understand what they are going to learn, practise or create. Where appropriate they should be encouraged to plan their own work and at the end of a lesson they should reflect on what they know, understand and can do and to share the successes and difficulties they have encountered.

Provision for ICT is central to national policy initiatives for education. Standards for initial teacher training require all teachers to know when it is appropriate to use ICT in subject teaching. Current national policy intends that all maintained schools should be connected to the internet and the National Grid for Learning (NGfL). The NGfL provides funding for hardware, training and resources and access to software, content and services. Contributors to the NGfL include the government, public services, schools, the commercial sector, museums and libraries.

Supporting staff

It is important to recognise that not all adults will have e-confidence at a personal level. This includes teachers and support staff. When working with an ICT activity you may need to take into account considerations such as your own competence and confidence with the hardware and software, the complexity of the activity being set and your familiarity with it. You also need to consider the age, ability and expertise of the learners you are supporting and the amount of assistance they will require. It is advisable to identify key ideas and questions that learners need to consider when looking at the planning process and to incorporate feedback at the end of a lesson to inform future provision. Professional development in ICT is very important and the appraisal process can be used to identify personal training and development needs.

Task 7F

Conduct a SWOT (Strengths, Weaknesses, Opportunities and Threats) analysis of your personal knowledge, skills and understanding in ICT.
How does this relate to any personal or professional development action plans you may have?

Managing Data

There are many opportunities for learners, support staff and teachers to use computers and software in their work. ICT can be used to enable organisations collect, keep, use and present data. For example one key area where ICT can play a key role is in the management of assessment data. ICT can be used to collect a range of information statistics such as attendance information or test results. Such data can be interrogated quickly and used to inform future teaching. Thus information can be held and stored efficiently and be recalled easily allowing users to call up information in a variety of formats. Particular software programs enable users to predict quikly future trends and engage in developments based on a whole range of information. Using ICT enables organisations to present data in multiple ways dependent upon the audience and make such information easily accessible to all staff. For example, the storage of data on a central server accessible through a network means that staff can access assessment data from the classroom.

The accessibility of data leaves us with some issues to consider. Some data, such as data referring to individual pupils, must be held securely and with protocols for access to it. The accuracy of data is reliant on the person who enters the data onto the computer. Inaccuracy here renders the information held of little benefit as it would be unreliable. There are issues of staff training in relation to the use of ICT for the management of data as well as issues in relation to staffing as these forms of data management and storage expand. Careful thought must be given to what data needs to be kept and how it will be used and accessed if the system is to be robust in supporting teaching and learning. There is a risk that the computer may become an 'electronic filing cabinet' where data is stored but never used.

Health and safety

There are health and safety issues in relation to the use of ICT within the workplace. These apply to adults using ICT to carry out their job and to learners using ICT. The workplace will have a health and safety policy. References to health and safety will also be found in the ICT policy. All staff should know how to minimise risks and to encourage the safe use of ICT equipment. There should be appropriate lighting in the room and ICT activities should not last for excessive periods of time without an alternative activity or break being included as part of the session. Some health problems may be triggered by computer screens and in addition seating should be appropriate to prevent back injuries. As with any electrical equipment care should be taken. Furthermore there are legal considerations relating to the Data Protection Act and copyright legislation. For example, ethical issues, including access to illegal or unsuitable materials on the internet, must be considered. This includes a whole gamut of consideration such as the acknowledgment of sources, confidentiality of personal data and the ways in which users can be monitored. These are usually identified in policy documents.

Teaching and learning

Effective teaching and learning in ICT is accomplished through making use of a range of approaches. Whole-class teaching using a large monitor or projector may be appropriate for teaching skills, introducing lessons, reinforcement during lessons and as a conclusion to lessons or as a plenary session. Usually in ICT learners will work individually, in pairs or in small groups. Individual work enables learners to develop their own skills or personal ideas whereas paired work promotes learner interaction and discussion around the problem posed, thus learners provide each other with peer support. It may also be necessary for learners to share access to resources. Group work is useful during simulations or modelling activities, as in these situations discussion is an important part of the learning. As with other subjects, quality teaching and learning in ICT is achieved through the careful identification of learning objectives which take account of learners' existing IT capabilities to ensure progression. There should be structured planning that lies within the school IT policy to ensure this continuity. Lessons need to be dynamic and should demonstrate a good match between the teaching strategy and the intended learning outcomes. It is also important that a range of differentiated teaching and learning activities are used. The following themes are indicative of the effective teaching of ICT:

- Supporting good practice
- Setting high expectations
- Having clear objectives
- Using a variety of teaching methods and strategies
- Modelling effective behaviours
- Providing 'authentic' experiences
- Supporting collaboration
- Assisting the management of learning

- Managing learning
- Using a range of assessment methods
- Providing feedback
- Supporting planning
- Managing time and pace well
- Promoting an Effective Learning Environment
- Creating an effective learning environment
- Extending beyond the lesson
- Celebrating success
- Teamwork and relating to others

(BECTa 2002)

ICT can be used to provide differentiation. Differentiation is the process through which a school can plan appropriately challenging work that meets the needs of individuals/ groups/whole class. There are some key ways of differentiating. These are summarised in Figure 7.2.

We can differentiate within the ICT curriculum to meet the needs of all learners. For learners with SEN (special educational needs) ICT is a powerful tool. Learners can use ICT to edit and amend their work and produce written work to a high standard. ICT can provide opportunities to work collaboratively or alone and it can be used to motivate disaffected learners. Many ICT applications allow for immediate feedback to learners often presented as a game or a challenge. There is software available that is designed to appeal to learners with specific needs, learners of a specific age and designed to capture the learner's attention for an extended period of time. In addition, activities can be broken down into small supportive steps. Many applications have additional benefits such as the use of synthesised speech. ICT can also help learners who are studying English as an Additional Language by providing opportunities for language exploration. Consequently, ICT can be an extremely useful tool that can help address the learning needs of many different types of learner.

Figure 7.2 Ways of differentiating

Task	matching different tasks to learners' abilities
Support	offering additional adult or peer assistance
Time	giving more/less time to complete a task
Outcome	reducing the number of tasks, and the amount or quality of work required
Presentation	using different media to present ideas
Content	choosing different content according to the needs of the learner
Resource	using different resources that support learners' needs
Grouping	putting learners' into groups of similar ability allows for targeted support

Conclusion

This chapter has provided you with a basic introduction to the ICT curriculum and has provided you with some guidelines for good practice in relation to the teaching and learning of ICT. This curriculum area is dynamic, is constantly developing and has a variety of uses.

As a result it is advisable to check websites and publications for up-to date-information on research information in this area. New opportunities to communicate and access information mean that IT can be viewed as an enabling technology in terms of supporting learning. This is particularly relevant for learners with SEN. As a result, all those working in education should be aware of the potential uses of ICT for themselves and for their learners. To learn more look through the next section for books to follow up.

📖 Bibliography

BECTa (2002) 'ICT supporting teaching: developing effective practice' http://www.becta.org.uk/subsections/awards/practice_awards/documents/effectivepractice.pdf

Beynon, J. and Mackay, H. (1989) 'Information technology into education: towards a critical perspective', *Journal of Education Policy*, 4(3), 245–57.

Copyright Licensing Act 2000.

Data Protection Act 1998.

DfEE (1998) *ICT: A Scheme of Work for Key Stages 1 and 2*, London: DfEE.

DfEE (1999) *The National Curriculum Handbook for Primary Teachers in England*, London: DfEE.

DfES (2000) *Curriculum Guidance for the Foundation Stage*, London: DfES.

Kemmis, S., Atkin, R. and Wright, E. (1977) *How do Students Learn? Working papers on Computer-Assisted Learning*, Norwich: Norwich Centre for Applied Research in Education, University of East Anglia.

NCSL (2004) 'Strategic leadership of ICT', http://www.ncsl.org.uk/slict.

Papert, S. (1980) *Mindstorms: Children, Computers and Powerful Ideas*, New York: Basic Books.

Chapter 8

Behaviour management

This chapter sets out to discuss the concepts and issues surrounding behaviour management. At present, England and Wales seem to have an obsession about the behaviour of children with an explosion of television programmes such as 'Super Nanny' and 'Little Angels' which focus on the 'best' way to correct inappropriate behaviour (www.viewingfigures.com). In each episode, behavioural gurus address the problem of correcting the behaviour of children with arguably increasingly greater emotional and behavioural difficulties. Educators draw attention to levels of poor behaviour, low concentration and aggression in children. Whilst media attention is often directed at poor behaviour in schools related to areas of socio-economic deprivation, even schools in more affluent areas note how children are continually pushing the boundaries with unwanted remarks and an increased lack of respect. Many books concentrate on this one theme. This chapter does not aim to discuss or debate the history of behaviour management nor claim to provide a remedy for unwanted behaviour in schools. We do however highlight current practices in behaviour management and aim to explore the existing range of strategies that practitioners utilise. We have divided this chapter into three sections: common forms of unwanted behaviour (and the reasons for them); ways of managing behaviour and bullying; and finally we explore the issue of self-esteem.

Common forms of unwanted behaviour

Unwanted behaviour can encompass a variety of forms, from someone shouting out in a classroom to someone displaying severe aggression. Unwanted behaviour may simply be displaying a 'normal' behaviour in an inappropriate place, at an inappropriate time, or with an inappropriate person, for example when a learner is referring to a teacher using inappropriate language. In this part of the chapter we will discuss, identify and begin to offer some explanations about why these different forms of unwanted behaviour may be present.

Expected Levels of Behaviour

Task 8A

What forms of unwanted behaviour have you seen in the classroom?
Are they all severe types of disruption / misbehaviour?

We all have views on what constitutes appropriate behaviour that are based on our experiences from childhood through to adulthood. Consequently, we all have an opinion about how children should behave. The topic of behaviour can become the focus of heated debate! We only need to observe parents of small children in a supermarket on a busy Saturday morning. A child may have a tantrum in the middle of the shop floor because they want a bar of chocolate that the parent is refusing to buy. The child shouts, screams and cries until almost all in the shop have noticed what is going on. What does the parent do? What choices can they make? In this situation the parent might choose one of several options. They may for example:

 Ignore the child.
 Smack the child.
 Buy the bar of chocolate.

Obviously there are more choices the parent could make; however, on a Saturday morning and to many parents these may be the only options they feel they have. Whatever option they choose, however, others will disagree. We have all seen such an example and mutter to ourselves about what the parent should be doing. What we need to consider though is that it is neither the outcome nor the intervention that is the issue. What we need to focus on is what level of behaviour is expected from that child. What has been set as the level of behaviour expected in the past? Does the child know they are misbehaving? Is this behaviour so common that the parent now treats it as the norm? Once these issues are understood then appropriate intervention techniques can be introduced.

Factors to consider

Applying discipline and the use of intervention programmes are only preliminary steps in the behaviour management framework. Understanding the possible reasons for such behaviour must also be explored in a bid to manage successfully and resolve the problems. In other words, different individuals will have different reasons for inappropriate behaviour and therefore the responses to it and understandings of it will need to vary accordingly. Examples of these different reasons could include: poor relationships within the family, trauma at home, low self-esteem, a death in the family, boredom at school, peer pressure. All of these examples would require taking a different approach. Therefore unwanted behaviour exists for a variety of reasons. The explanations and impacts on behaviour are endless but factors to consider may include:

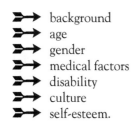

background
age
gender
medical factors
disability
culture
self-esteem.

All of the above will affect how we behave and be factors in the formation of our character and opinions. When considering 'background' we need to identify the factors that may be present in the background of a learner's life. Whilst many of these will be unalterable it is important to understand their impact and could include parenting style, family make-up or construction, place in the family, socio-economic status and geographical location. The age of the learner will have an impact in terms of their developmental stage physically, emotionally and socially. For example, a young child may have had an early growth spurt and be bullied because of their height, a learner may have a problem with controlling their anger or they may not be able to function with others their own age. Gender may also impact upon behaviour partly as a response to biological differences but also as a result of the pressures of society. Peer pressure from boys might contribute to violence in an attempt to demonstrate superior masculinity. Similarly, adolescent girls often try to wear inappropriate clothing in an attempt to conform to societal images of young women. For further discussion of the impact of gender on education see Chapter 12.

We all exist within a multiple set of cultures which dictate norms of behaviour. Some of these cultures may operate differently to each other so the same behaviour is viewed differently under different circumstances. For example, there may be a mismatch between the values of home and the values of school which some learners find difficult to understand. It may be difficult for instance if a learner comes from a very easy-going home to handle a classroom dominated by an authoritarian teacher. Different families may operate different cultures and routines to one another, such as whether the family sit together at meal times, or whether the learner is expected to apply themselves to their school work. Religious beliefs and customs can also affect behaviour. Some religions require adherence to religious practices that fall outside of western cultural norms practised in schools and colleges. For example, Muslim learners may need time to pray whilst Jehovah's Witnesses require absence from religious education studies and assemblies. There has been recent publicity involving conflicts about incompatibilities between religious and school dress codes. Thus issues such as where a learner lives and the groups they belong to are important to consider.

All of these issues, together with many more, will have a lot to do with the shaping of behaviour and may make a learner feel different from their peers. Some differences may impact on the self-confidence of a learner or may even result in situations of bullying or being bullied. We will now discuss some specific disorders that learners may display.

Emotional and Behavioural Difficulties

Emotional and Behavioural Difficulties (EBD) is a general term. The definition of EBD articulated in Circular 9/94 (DfEE 1994) and contained in the DfES document *The Special*

Educational Needs Code of Practice (2001), suggests that EBD may become apparent in the following ways:

➤ age-inappropriate behaviour or that which seems otherwise socially inappropriate or strange behaviour which interferes with the learning of the pupil or their peers
➤ signs of emotional turbulence (e.g. unusual tearfulness, withdrawal from social situations)
➤ difficulties in forming and maintaining positive relationships.

Emotional and behavioural difficulties can be viewed as a continuum from infrequent episodes of problematic behaviour to more persistent problems which indicate an underlying medical or psychiatric condition. It is important not to use the label 'EBD' to explain infrequent behavioural symptoms in learners. It should be used only when the problems of behaviour are severe enough to impact on the learner's development and education.

Attention deficit hyperactivity disorder

Attention deficit hyperactivity disorder (ADHD) is a disorder of childhood and adolescence characterised by a lack of impulse control, the inability to concentrate and hyperactivity. It is also called attention deficit disorder (ADD) when the hyperactivity is not present. Around one in twenty students (Lowey 2002) have ADD or ADHD in the UK. To be diagnosed with ADD/ADHD requires professional intervention which is normally obtained through the SEN Code of Practice (2001) or through medical referral. Where a diagnosis is obtained through medical referral alone (often the case with children under five), the learner may also require the operation of the SEN Code of Practice (2001) as a result of the impact that behaviour has on learning. A school, teacher or parent cannot diagnose the condition. Although there is no agreement on the specific causes of AD /ADHD it is thought that the condition can either be attributed to a hereditary or genetic cause or to in-utero damage to the brain of the foetus during pregnancy or damage to the brain at or after birth (www.bbc.co.uk). Common traits of the condition are summarised by Lowey (2002):

➤ often fidgets with hands or feet or squirms in seats
➤ has difficulty in remaining seated
➤ is easily distracted by external stimuli
➤ has difficulty awaiting turns in group situations
➤ often blurts out answers before they have been completed
➤ has difficulty in following through instructions (not due to oppositional behaviour or failure of comprehension)
➤ has difficulty in sustaining attention in tasks and play activities
➤ often shifts from one uncompleted activity to another
➤ has difficulty playing quietly
➤ often talks excessively
➤ often interrupts or intrudes on others
➤ often does not seem to listen to what is being said to them
➤ often loses things necessary for tasks and activities at school or at home

➤➤ often engages in physically dangerous activities without considering the possible consequences

Many learners demonstrate a number of these traits. However this does not mean that they all have ADD/ADHD. Learners with this condition will demonstrate most of the traits simultaneously in one or more situations. In some cases, medication such as Ritalin may be prescribed (Frederickson and Cline 2002). It is not a condition that a child will grow out of. It is not a 'phase' but a serious medical condition. Supporting learners with ADD / ADHD is a hard task. Strategies to manage the behaviour and associated learning difficulties need to be implemented. An Educational Psychologist will certainly be involved in the process of diagnosis and support and a Individual Behavioural Plan (BEP) will be written which identifies weakness and strengths and outlines the support available. The plan will act in the same way as an Individual Education Plan (IEP). Some schools prefer not to use the term BEP and use IEP.

Autism

Autism is a developmental disability that typically appears during the first three years of life. It is a result of a neurological disorder that affects the functioning of the brain. There is no known single cause for autism but it is generally accepted that it is related to abnormalities in brain structure or function. These may occur as a result of birth trauma. There also appears to be a genetic basis to the disorder. Autism tends to occur more frequently than expected among individuals who have certain medical conditions, including Fragile X syndrome and congenital rubella syndrome. Some harmful substances ingested during pregnancy have also have been associated with an increased risk of autism. The question of a relationship between vaccines and autism continues to be debated. Autism impacts upon the normal development of the brain in the areas of social interaction and communication skills. Autistic individuals have difficulties in verbal and non-verbal communication, social interactions and leisure or play activities. Persons with autism may also exhibit some of the following traits:

➤➤ Insistence on sameness
➤➤ Resistance to change
➤➤ Difficulty in expressing needs
➤➤ Use of gestures or pointing instead of words
➤➤ Repeats words or phrases
➤➤ Laughing, crying or showing distress for reasons not apparent to others
➤➤ Prefers to be alone
➤➤ Tantrums
➤➤ Difficulty in mixing with others
➤➤ Dislikes physical attention
➤➤ Little or no eye contact
➤➤ Unresponsive to normal teaching methods
➤➤ Sustained odd play
➤➤ Inappropriate attachments to objects
➤➤ Over-sensitivity

➤➤ Under-sensitivity to pain
➤➤ No real fears of danger
➤➤ Noticeable physical over-activity
➤➤ Extreme under-activity
➤➤ Uneven gross/fine motor skills
➤➤ Not responsive to verbal cues

Autism occurs throughout the world in families of all racial, ethnic and social backgrounds. What must be remembered is that Autism is treatable and that early diagnosis and intervention are vital to the future development of the child.

Asperger's Syndrome

Asperger's Syndrome is usually thought of as a condition on the autistic spectrum. Asperger's Syndrome is a neurobiological disorder identified by Hans Asperger in 1944. Asperger published a paper which described a pattern of behaviours in young boys who had normal intelligence and language development, but who also exhibited autistic-like behaviours and marked deficiencies in social and communication skills. In spite of the publication of his paper in the 1940s, it wasn't until 1994 that Asperger's Syndrome has been recognised by medical professionals.

A person with Asperger's Syndrome perceives the world differently. The behaviours they display that seem odd or unusual are due to neurological differences. Often these behaviours are attributed to intentional rudeness, poor behaviour and poor parenting by those witnessing an incident. Individuals with Asperger's Syndrome exhibit a variety of characteristics and the disorder can range from mild to severe. There may be marked deficiencies in social skills, difficulties with transitions or change. Obsessive routines and preoccupation with particular subjects are common traits. Learners with Asperger's Syndrome have difficulty reading nonverbal cues (body language) and using body space. They can be overly sensitive to sounds, tastes, smells and sights.

Bullying

This area of behaviour has been of popular concern over the last few years. Many initiatives have been implemented to raise awareness of the issue. For example, the BBC released blue 'beat bullying' wrist bands as part of a national campaign, wearers demonstrating their awareness of the need to 'stamp out' bullying in schools and sports. Bullying is repeated harassment over a period of time. It is done in a way that makes it difficult for the person being bullied to defend themselves.

We can identify three main types of bullying: verbal, physical and indirect bullying. Verbal bullying includes:

➤➤ Teasing
➤➤ Sarcasm
➤➤ Name calling
➤➤ Continually ignoring someone
➤➤ Racist remarks
➤➤ Sexist remarks

Physical bullying includes:

- Taking money or personal belongings
- Pushing, hitting, kicking and punching
- Sexual abuse, including unwanted physical contact and/or comments

Indirect bullying includes:

- Spreading rumours or starting gossip
- Getting someone into trouble for no real reason
- Excluding someone
- Sending hurtful messages via texts, e-mails, the phone and letters

Bullying can be overt or covert and difficult to detect. Some victims are good at hiding what is happening. Bullying can happen anywhere and anyone can become the victim of a bully. Schools have a duty under the Education Act (2002) to 'safeguard and promote the welfare of children' (Section 175) and should be alert to the issue of bullying. Identifying someone who has become the victim of bullying is not always easy. However there are a number of symptoms that can indicate a learner is suffering from bullying such as a sudden change in their behaviour, becoming depressed or withdrawn, avoiding college or school for no obvious reason, being happy in some contexts but unhappy in others and/or unexplained bruises, scratches or any other physical injuries.

Ways of managing behaviour

Managing behaviour requires a planned approach and dedication by all parties involved. Educators employ a whole range of behaviour strategies that address behaviour at different levels for different audiences. For example they may offer incentives such as student of the week for effort, longer playtimes if a whole class improves their behaviour in assemblies and individual target sheets for children needing extra attention. Unknown to many are the theories that lie behind many of these strategies. In essence – why do they work?

Behaviourist approaches

Task 8B

Consider the following quotation.

> A person behaves in a certain way because he has been taught or because he has not been taught to behave differently.
>
> (Westmacott and Cameron 1981)

Do you agree or disagree with this statement?
Can you support your view with reference to observations from the workplace?

Many strategies rely on work completed by behavioural theorists. Behaviourists believe that behaviours are learned from the environment and from others around us. Patterns of behaviour that learners have seen and encountered will impact on their own behaviour. Behaviour theories are strongly based on Classical Conditioning and Operant Conditioning. Classical conditioning is where a particular stimulus is associated with a particular condition.

> A conditioned stimulus elicits an unconditioned response. For example: a ringing bell elicits attention. An unconditioned stimulus elicits an unconditioned response. For example: food is continually presented after the bell is rung and elicits salivation. Finally the conditioned stimulus elicits the conditioned response. For example: the bell soon elicits salivation on its own.
>
> (Ayers *et al.* 1995: 12)

Operant conditioning is heavily related to the responses to particular behaviours. An example would be using positive reinforcement to establish good behaviour and the provision of negative reinforcement for unwanted behaviour. Therefore we learn about unwanted behaviour by observing and experiencing responses to our behaviours from others. This also explains why peer pressure can lead to poor behaviour as such activities can be reinforced through the ability to impress the peer group.

Consequently, behaviourism is fundamentally concerned with actual physical behaviour itself and not the emotion, thinking or attitudes that underlie that behaviour. In this respect it treats all learners as if they were the same irrespective of other factors, such as background. It assumes that if we are all subject to the same conditioning approaches we will all respond similarly. Thus behaviourist approaches to problems will include:

- Positive reinforcements – When an individual has displayed appropriate behaviour they are praised for it. This offering of praise and reward encourages good behaviour to continue. Montgomery (1989) extended this approach to include the 'catch them being good' theory, which allowed educators to look purposefully for good behaviour in learners and thus begin a positive reinforcement strategy which makes the learner feel good about themselves.
- Token economy (Ayers *et al.* 1995) – This approach adopts some 'credit card' type of system whereby the learner receives tokens or credits for positive behaviour that are accumulated and exchanged for rewards. The tokens must be awarded as soon as the desired behaviour is displayed – this immediate acknowledgement reinforces the good behaviour and is widely adopted in schools.
- Time outs – 'Time outs' are used to isolate individuals from the rest of the learning group. Time outs mean that the learner is excluded or removed from his or her peers for a set amount of time. This means that learners cannot interfere with the wider group, nor can they earn rewards (Ayers *et al.* 1995). This allows frustrated learners the time to cool down and reflect on their behaviour. However, this is of secondary benefit in behaviourist theory terms as it is the direct link between 'time out' and the negative sanction for unwanted behaviour that is regarded to be the key. Some learners are given the opportunity to select their own 'time out' but they can 'play the system'. Once they are unhappy in a lesson, or have decided that they don't want to take part in it they take a 'time out'. This can disrupt their own learning and that of others in the class.

Time out is a form of isolation. Isolation is possibly the harshest punishment that we can prescribe both in school and in society. Think of convicted criminals – we isolate them from society. When in prison and not conforming to rules and regulations prisoners are placed in solitary confinement – isolation at its extreme. The test of behaviour management theories must be whether or not they work on 'the shop floor' – do they work in the classroom? Possibly the hardest thing about behaviourist approaches in the classroom is the consistency that is needed. In behaviourist approaches learners need tight boundaries, targets and a clear understanding of what is acceptable and what is not. Consistency is vital and the same praise and sanctions need to be applied whenever learners behave appropriately or inappropriately. It is this consistency that is hard to maintain in a classroom or organisational context as all staff need to deliver rewards and sanctions in the same way.

 Task 8C

Can you think of behaviour/reward strategies which were too onerous on teaching staff and consequently have not worked?

Consider the following. In a primary class the children's reading records need to be signed by a parent or guardian at home every night. It is usually one of the TA's tasks to check that all are signed. If a child's book is signed they get a sticker on a chart – twenty stickers means they are allowed ten minutes free time on the computer. For two days the class teacher is ill and the head has asked the TA to cover the class using planning completed prior to the absence by the class teacher. In essence this is positive reinforcement and a token reward system – hence the reinforcement needs to be carried out every day. In this case the TA will have more than enough tasks to carry out without having to check every reading record – as would a teacher if they were alone for two days. The reading record is not checked and the stickers are not allocated. What message does the child gain as a result of this inconsistency? This is a good example of where this type of conditioning requires a consistency which has to be planned for and a lot of effort is necessary to be directed into it for it to be sustained. As a consequence these types of behavioural approach need all staff to support them.

Cognitive approaches to behaviour

Cognitive approaches focus centrally on the individual's perceptions of their own and others' behaviour (Fredrickson and Cline 2002). Unlike behaviourist approaches, they take into consideration the attitudes and beliefs of the learner. This means that an individual approach to behaviour intervention must be considered.

 Task 8D

A teacher sees two learners talking during a class test and gives them both a time out.
Will they both interpret the punishment and react in the same way?
If not why not?

In the case above behaviourist theories would assume that both learners will react similarly to the punishment and acknowledge their own guilt. This approach does not, however, acknowledge their individual perceptions of the situation. For example one learner may feel that they weren't talking but simply responding to the other person and therefore express resentment towards the teacher. Cognitive theory acknowledges this difference in attitudes that learners will have when reflecting on their behaviour.

Cognitive theorists also recognise the concept that learners may not be able to perceive the meaning of the behaviour of others. For example in a school there may be a particular child who always ends up being upset and fighting other children in the playground. Why? One theory is that these children cannot interpret the behaviour of others fully. Hence their response is triggered by the reptilian part of their brain and enters the 'fight or flight' receptors – thus the child is forced, by reaction, to fight or flee the situation (Frederickson and Cline 2002). Cognitive approaches to problems may include:

➤➤ Reflection tasks for the learner to complete which will indicate their feelings, perceptions and attitudes towards their own behaviour.
➤➤ Discussions with learning mentors about how they perceive the behaviour of others toward them.
➤➤ School links with parents to identify the child's behavioural development (Ayers *et al.* 1995).
➤➤ Learners creating their own targets and being in charge of their own decisions – e.g. selective time out.

As before, we need to consider the pros and cons of these approaches on the 'shop floor'. Do they work in a learning environment?

The problem with these approaches, like behaviourist approaches, is that they take time. Additionally, cognitive approaches need to take account of the fact that some of the behaviour of the learner has been built up over time and will not be solved overnight. Reflection is a difficult skill to acquire and needs to be taught particularly where reflecting on behaviour involves challenging reactions learned over a long period of time. It may be that the learner can do no more than identify where the problems are and the educator supports this by developing an understanding about why the behaviour response has been triggered. This is a time-consuming process. In the classroom educators may find it hard to find the time to work on such programmes. For others this approach is based upon a 'softly softly' approach and they find it difficult to accept an approach to behaviour management which accords more attention to the learner with unwanted behaviour than that received by other learners within the same setting. In summary, like behaviourist approaches, consistency and effort by all parties are necessary to ensure that these behaviour management strategies work. Also, because both have advantages and disadvantages as strategies we often see a mixture of behaviourist and cognitive approaches used in parallel to manage behaviour.

Psychodynamic and systemic approaches

Psychodynamic and systemic behaviour are two other theories which can be used to explain the behaviour of learners in the classroom. Psychodynamic approaches acknowledge that the desires, drives and fantasies affecting behaviour are unconscious and result in the possibility that the individual suffers from intense feelings that they cannot always understand (Frederickson and Cline 2002). Systemic approaches highlight the problems that learners face in the interpretation of the rules and routines of the different behaviour management systems present in a learning environment. They also highlight the potential competition and confusion between family systems, school systems and peer group systems.

Discipline policies and procedures

Each organisation will endorse its own discipline policies and procedures. These will probably be an amalgamation of strategies that have been proven by experience to work. Many will have a rigorous set of procedures for behaviour. Consider the following examples.

➤➤ In a primary school there may be a traffic light system: Children's names are placed on a colour coded chart: green for good, amber for 'could do better', red for poor behaviour. The children can work their way into the green by applying the correct behaviour. These types of systems can be recorded and linked to rewards and sanctions.

➤➤ In a secondary school there may be a Card system: similar to soccer – yellow cards are warnings; red cards trigger a sanction.

➤➤ In any setting there may be a progressive warning system where learners are required to understand what each warning means. If they display inappropriate behaviour they are warned. Warnings and associated sanctions become progressively harsher. A simple progressive warning system is outlined in Figure 8.1.

In systems like the one shown in Figure 8.1, obvious variations in sanctions and levels exist but they all share the common theme of exclusion from the learning group. An additional theme is the ultimate sanction of removal from the organisation. In the primary and secondary school it is necessary to get parents to support the system of sanctions. Lack of either parental support or the enforcement of sanctions renders the system ineffective and unsupportive of a learning environment. Systems of sanction should give clear guidance

---

Task 8E

Do you recognise any of the types of policies?
What do you think are the main strengths and weakness of them?
Motivation and rewards have not been mentioned in the examples given.
What, and how, would you integrate motivation and rewards into the examples given?

Figure 8.1 Progressive warnings

Warning Number	Sanction
1	Verbal Warning
2	Time out in class room
3	Extended time out in a different room
4	Excluded from class for the day
5	Excluded from establishment

to both learners and teachers who then both know what level of behaviour is expected. The teacher can then use the system to direct behaviour effectively.

Self-esteem

The importance of self-esteem can be traced back to Maslow's hierarchy of needs (Roffey and O'Reirdan 1997). Maslow identified that all humans have fundamental needs which can be placed in a hierarchical order of importance. (See also Chapter 3). These are:

- Physiological or survival needs
- Safety needs – shelter
- Love, affection and belonging
- Self-esteem
- Self-actualisation

(Roffey and O'Reirdan 1997)

Maslow's work impacts on our understanding of behaviour. For example, if a learner does not feel safe this will impact on their ability to fulfil other needs and may negatively affect their behaviour. Self-esteem is more than just feeling good about ourselves. Self-esteem can be seen as central to our development. It is not only linked with behaviour but also attainment (Roffey and O'Reirdan 1997). As adults we know that when we feel good about ourselves we achieve better results. Conversely, when we 'get out of the wrong side of bed' everything seems to go wrong. When our self-esteem is high we tend to treat mistakes as part of a learning curve, rather than as a failure. When self-esteem is low the opposite

---

Task 8F

Think of a learner that you see exhibiting low self-esteem.
What traits do they show of this e.g. isolation, shyness etc.
How is this addressed by staff?

---

occurs. Learners with low self-esteem can feel frustrated, isolated and depressed. They feel that every move they make contributes to the poor performance they are producing. Even if the performance is not that low, they may still perceive it as such.

When learners are suffering from low self-esteem, it may be necessary to introduce targeted intervention. Low self-esteem might mean the learner is withdrawn but can also lead to outbursts of frustration and anger which can escalate into conflict. Having a good relationship with a learner with low self-esteem is a helpful foundation from which to raise their confidence. As adults we should be aware that forgetting someone's name may be disappointing. We would not relish the idea of someone in authority over us not being aware of who we are. The same is true of learners and the simple act of recalling a name or a fact about them will raise their self-esteem. With children this may be asking them about a hobby or how their favourite football team is performing. Sometimes it will require a more sustained effort upon the part of the adult. For example, a learner may be suffering from low self-esteem due to having a smaller physical frame than their peers and may as a result be quiet and withdrawn. As an educator you may observe that the learner loves comics. By purposefully taking the time to discuss the latest issue of that comic you can show that you are taking an interest in the learner. This may necessitate you taking some of your time to find out more about the learner but the effort is well worth it as they will become accustomed to your interest and may even begin to initiate conversations themselves. The following interventions have been identified by Roffey and O'Reirdan (1997) as helpful in raising self-esteem:

➤➤ Include gender and racial issues within the class, e.g. getting local community speakers in of different genders and races
➤➤ Don't create 'self-fulfilling prophecies' e.g. 'this is the untidiest classroom I have come across' – if it is that bad, why should anyone bother to change it?
➤➤ Criticise the behaviour of learners as poor, not the learners themselves
➤➤ Try not to compare learners, especially siblings
➤➤ Praise and say positive things wherever possible

Task 8G

Think about Roffey and O'Reirdan's examples.
Which of these have you seen?
What other strategies have you seen?
How effective were they?

Many of these statements make 'common sense'; however, with so much going on in the classroom at such a quick pace it is easy to forget.

Some strategies you might have witnessed and which give positive messages follow.

➤➤ In a primary school - when letting children leave the class for the weekend, tell them something they have to pass on to their parents – e.g. 'Tell mum that Mr. Hutchins is especially happy with the way you have sat in assembly this week' or 'I want your Gran to know how hard you've tried in maths this week, well done'. Certificates can be given out too.
➤➤ In an infant's class – at circle time pass around a box, telling the children it contains the most precious thing in the world. Inform them they must look inside the box, but not reveal its contents. When the children look inside, they find a mirror, showing their reflection.
➤➤ In secondary school – In PSHE, choose a learner to write a testimony about. The learner leaves the room. The teacher acts as scribe. All the other learners in turn, say something good, notable or positive about their classmate such as s/he is a good friend, always makes me smile, is a fast runner. When it is done, the learner re-enters the room. The teacher reads back what has been said.
➤➤ In College – Students are nominated by staff and by their peers for learners' awards. They receive public recognition for their learning.

Conclusion

In this chapter we have looked at behaviour management. We have identified and evaluated the theoretical underpinning of some common behaviour management strategies and discussed their effectiveness. We have seen that whilst inappropriate behaviour may be demonstrated within an education environment the cause of that behaviour may lie outside the organisation. We have also discussed the importance of continuity and consistency in dealing with inappropriate behaviour and the difficulties of achieving this in our daily practice. If you would like to find out more the Bibliography will help you.

   Bibliography

Asperger, H. (1944) 'Die "Autistischen Psychopathen"', *Kindesalter: Archiv für Psychiatrie und Nervenkrankheiten*, 117, 76–136.

Ayers, H., Clarke, D. and Murray, A. (1995) *Perspectives on Behaviour*, London: David Fulton.

BBC. Beat Bullying website, http://www.bbc.co.uk/radio1/onelife/personal/bullying/bullying_facts.shtml#affected.

BBC. Beat Bullying website, http://www.viewingfigures.com.

DfES (2001) *The Special Educational Needs Code of Practice*, London: HMSO.

Frederickson, N. and Cline, T. (2002) *Special Educational Needs, Inclusion and Diversity*, Buckingham: Open University Press.

Kanner, L. (1943) 'Autistic disturbances of affective contact', *Nervous Child*, 2, 217–50.

Montgomery, D. (1989) *Managing Behaviour Problems*, London: Hodder and Stoughton.

Roffey, S. and O'Reirdan, T. (1997) *Infant Classroom Behaviour: Needs, Perspectives and Strategies*, London: David Fulton Publishers.

Westmacott, E.V.S. and Cameron, R.J. (1981) *Behaviour Can Change*, London: Macmillan Education.

Chapter 9

Inclusive education

In this chapter we set out to discuss the concepts and issues surrounding Inclusive Education. The chapter is split into three sections beginning with discussion about Inclusive Education and the history of Special Educational Needs (SEN). We then move on to look at the Code of Practice and finally consider common forms of Special Educational Needs.

Inclusive education and the recent history of Special Educational Needs

Children have special educational needs if they have a learning difficulty which calls for special educational provision to be made for them. Children have a learning difficulty if they:

(a) have a significantly greater difficulty in learning than the majority of children of the same age; or

(b) have a disability which prevents or hinders them from making use of educational facilities of a kind generally provided for children of the same age in schools within the area of the local education authority

(c) are under compulsory school age and fall within the definition at (a) or (b) above or would so do if special educational provision was not made for them.

(DfES 2001:6)

The guidelines above demonstrate the very wide definition of Special Educational Needs (SEN). The scope of the definition incorporates all types of difficulties learners may have, from dyslexia to dyspraxia. To label a learner as having SEN is not very informative. To an extent we may all have Special Educational Needs of one kind or another. For example, we may have poor handwriting and trouble with spelling. The important difference between the general population and those diagnosed as SEN is the severity of the needs. The SEN Code of Practice (2001) applies to children. However, discussions about the nature of special educational needs and the ways in which organisations meet the needs of learners with SEN extends into all educational settings.

Gifted and talented

In general when we discuss SEN we tend to refer to children experiencing difficulties with learning and low attainment. SEN however can apply to any learner and it is important to make sure that we understand that the SEN category applies to learners at both ends of the academic scale. Consider the needs of gifted and talented learners. Those who are gifted academically may need additional support and targeted intervention from teaching staff in order to keep their minds challenged and interested. The problems that can occur with learners with low attainment such as poor behaviour, boredom and lack of respect, that may be due to not being able to access the curriculum or linked to the fact that the curriculum is not suitable for them, can all occur with gifted learners for the same reasons. We cannot expect gifted learners to 'toe the line' and have their needs ignored. We can, however, employ a variety of interventions. A gifted learner may access some of the curriculum in classes for older learners. They may access a wider curriculum with specialist teachers or take examinations earlier than would normally be expected. Having their SEN identified ensures that they receive the most appropriate education for their needs. Talented learners are those possessing skills within the arts or physical education. Like gifted learners, arrangements need to be made in order for their educational entitlement to be reached.

The development of education for learners with SEN

Figure 9.1 shows recent historical highlights that have affected the development of SEN education.

The above is merely a snapshot of recent polices that have had a larger effect on how SEN is treated within Local Authorities and schools. This chapter will not provide a detailed historical overview of SEN education or policy. We will however, pause very briefly to highlight the impact that the Warnock Report (1978) has had on policy and practice. Despite many of the recommendations not being fully imposed until the 1981 Education Act, the Warnock Committee proposed some key changes to the way in which we conceptualise SEN. For example, prior to the report, learners were labelled as 'handicapped'. Warnock argued that learners don't easily fit into a prescribed category (the label had also come to be a form of verbal abuse) and therefore the term Special Educational Needs was suggested. This is demonstrated on many children's Individual Educational Plans (IEPs) where needs in more than one curriculum area are present. To indicate severity the categories of mild, moderate and severe are now used (Jenkinson 1997). These terms are used in the 'Statementing process' also introduced in the 1981 Education Act (Soan 2004).

What is Inclusive Education?

Inclusion is the process of including learners with SEN in mainstream education. It is not correct to refer to the term as integration. To simplify, integration refers more to the individual having to 'fit in', whilst inclusion models force the establishment to make extensive modifications to include the SEN learner. Inclusive Education would mean that the learner is included throughout the organisation and in all aspects of the curriculum (Frederickson and Cline 2002). Inclusion is a process which the whole organisation needs to be aware of and actively promote. Educational organisations should have an inclusive ethos within a broad and balanced curriculum. They require systems for early identification

Figure 9.1 History of SEN

The Warnock Report 1978	A committee chaired by Mary Warnock to investigate special education in schools claimed that 18% of mainstream children have a special educational need and that children's attainment was influenced by the child's background.
The Education Act 1981	Formalised the title Special Educational Needs (SEN). Changing assessment of diagnosing disability to SEN identification (Frederickson and Cline 2002). 'Statementing' process introduced (Soan 2004)
The Education Reform Act 1988	The introduction of the National Curriculum. Many felt that the demand to teach such a wide scope of subjects would be harmful to the education of SEN children.
The Education Act 1993	Introduction of the SEN Code of Practice and Statementing. 'Under the act, local education authorities (LEAs) and school governing bodies must have regard to an SEN code of practice, which sets out in detail how they are expected to carry out their duties. Since then, the concept of inclusion for pupils with SEN, as well as for others with particular needs, has been defined and amplified within the revised National Curriculum and in further guidance from the Department for Education and Skills (DfES)' (Ofsted 2004: 3). The act enforced schools to use a five-stage assessment process.
Special Education Needs and Disability Act (SENDA) 2001	Firmly placed SEN and disability discrimination awareness in mainstream education. Mainstream schools no longer able to decline a pupil into the schools because of SEN.
The Revised Code of Practice 2002	Similar content to the original; however, there were changes in response to the SENDA document. The revised Code replaced the five stage assessment pieces with three – School Action, School Action Plus and Statement

of barriers to inclusion and participation. 'They should also have high expectations and suitable targets for all' (DfES 2001: 3).

This clearly demonstrates how inclusive education affects the whole organisation and the curriculum. It also affects all staff and stakeholders. From Midday Assistants to the Chair of the Governing Body, the process must be agreed to and encouraged. To create an inclusive ethos all involved must see the benefits of inclusive education and be motivated to support it. It is incumbent upon those in positions of responsibility to ensure that others follow and understand inclusive education procedures. For example, a curriculum leader must encourage staff to plan creatively to include all learners in activities and expect all learners to achieve to their potential (DfES 2001b). Similarly, all learners in a school should be included on a residential trip irrespective of their particular SEN. To formalise such procedures the Special Educational Needs and Disability Act 2001 (SENDA) has made discriminating against a learner on such grounds unlawful. This piece of legalisation has massive implications for educational organisations. It has brought much more choice and power to parents and learners and is ensuring that all organisations are equipped to meet the needs of learners with SEN.

Task 9A

As a result of SENDA your organisation may have invested in building work to construct wheelchair ramps or sound systems for the hearing impaired etc.
Is your organisation fully inclusive of all learners?

Mixed opinions

There are disparate views on the benefits of inclusive education. We need to be clear about the arguments for including rather than excluding learners from mainstream education. Learners who are placed in special schools or units can be and often are seen as different. They can be labelled, discriminated against and treated without equal respect by all sectors in society. Excluding such learners can lead to them being segregated from society and perceived as different throughout their lives. Furthermore, adults can tend to focus on the needs of the learners rather than on their existing strengths. A dyslexic learner who finds writing almost impossible may have high levels of attainment in mathematics. A learner with SEN may feel very frustrated when their achievements in other curriculum areas are not recognised.

Task 9B

A class has a learner in a wheelchair. Soccer is on the PE timetable this term.
How will the learner be integrated into this part of the curriculum?

It is also important to recognise that there are those who argue passionately that learners with SEN should be taught separately and that they can thrive and achieve well in an environment especially designed for them but perform less well and are consequently less confident in mainstream education. Whatever position you adopt Inclusive Education is certainly a topic of great importance in the current political, social and educational climate. In the Five Year Strategy for Children and Learners (DfES 2004) the stated aim of Inclusive Education is to 'break down the divide between mainstream and special schools to create a unified system which meets the needs of all children' (DfES 2004: 37). It does not see the eradication of schools designed to meet the complex needs experienced by some learners. 'Special schools have an important role to play in educating those children with the most complex and severe special educational needs and in sharing their expertise with other schools to support inclusion' (ibid.: 37). The above statement must be read however with a critical eye. There is little clarification as to what is meant by the term 'children with the most complex and severe special education needs'. If we take the stance of assuming that this refers to learners with physical and mental difficulties, then learners with Moderate Learning Difficulties (MLD) would certainly be placed inside mainstream classrooms and not in a school for children with MLD. MLD schools typically have a lower class size than mainstream schools ensuring that children receive the maximum attention and intervention to meet their needs. Staff in MLD schools also have access to specific training. There are similar effects for those with an Emotional Behaviour Disorder Statement (EBD). These learners have a Statement, not necessarily through having low attainment academically, but as a result of inappropriate behaviour. Many believe that classroom disruption due to poor behaviour is bad enough as it is without the added burden of including more behaviourally challenged children into the classroom. It is also argued that those working in mainstream settings do not have appropriate expertise to meet the needs of these learners. Schools may attempt to include children by adapting the school, but how far can they go? Building work costs a lot of money. What about specialist staff? Mainstream teachers faced with MLD students within a class of 29 students may find the task of planning, preparing and assessing very difficult and certainly time constraining.

 Task 9C

Make a list of the positive and negative effects that Inclusive Education has on:
The learner
The organisation
Wider society

You may not have a clear-cut answer as to whether you agree or not with Inclusion polices, but as a professional you will need to develop your opinions on the subject.

The Code of Practice

The Code of Practice sets out guidance on policies and procedures 'aimed at enabling pupils with special educational needs (SEN) to reach their full potential, to be included fully in their school communities and make a successful transition to adulthood' (DfES 2001: 6 1:2). The Code, created in 1993 and revised in 2001, provides schools with guidance about how they can conform to the legislation when working with learners with SEN. The Code does not give guidance on specific subjects nor is it an optional strategy. It is legislation and must be adhered to by schools and Local Authorities (DfES 2001).

Identification and the school SEN register

Some learners are identified as having SEN before entry to school, for example, those with a physical disability. However, most will be identified during their time in education. Within mainstream schooling a teacher or TA may notice that a learner is experiencing falling or below average attainment or they may suspect that the learner has a specific learning need. This is then brought to the attention of the Special Educational Needs Co-ordinator (SENCO). The SENCO will review the learner and may ask the teacher or TA to monitor progress. If the SENCO thinks there is a problem or that there are specific difficulties they will place the learner on the SEN register. The SEN register is required by the Code of Practice. It contains the names of all the learners that the SENCO deems as needing support as a result of having SEN.

Task 9D

What percentage of your school's population is on the SEN register?

Levels of support

Figure 9.2 sets the Code's graduated approach to process SEN children from identification through to the process of statementing.

Individual Education Plans

An Individual Education Plan (IEP) is a plan that outlines the intervention necessary to support the learner's needs. IEPs look different according to the organisation that you work in. However they should all contain the following information

- ⮕ Weakness/difficulties – This is a list that clearly defines the main difficulties experienced by the learner
- ⮕ Targets – A short defined list of targets – usually short term (half termly) which the teacher has identified with the SENCO
- ⮕ Intervention/support – A list of support strategies, intervention programmes and resources to be used
- ⮕ Parents' comments – Parents should be invited into the school to discuss progress made towards IEP targets
- ⮕ Learner's comments – The Code stresses that learners should be aware of their IEP. They should be a part of devising the targets and aware of what is expected of them. They should also be able to make suggestions for the targets.

IEPs are not to be treated as continuing and continual paperwork. They are an additional task particularly in classrooms where several learners may be identified as having SEN but they should be considered as a tool to be used with all those involved in the learning process. They allow you to plan, record and monitor the success of interventions made in meeting the identified needs of the learner. They should be reviewed at least twice a year (DfES 2001). However, in practice they tend to be updated at least once a term. IEPs that sit at the back of a cupboard are not working documents and have little effect on the development of learning.

Figure 9.2 Graduated approach to process SEN children

Process	Stage	Likely outcomes
SEN suspected	Reviewed by the SENCO	
SEN identified	Placed on the school's SEN register at School Action (SA)	Usually learner and parents consulted. Creation, and constant revision of IEP '... additional and different approaches to learning arrangements normally provided for all children' (DfES 2001) Support given only by the school
Monitoring of learner		IEP reviewed
Assuming no or little progress is made	Moved to School Action Plus (SA+)	Schools request additional support from outside agencies- e.g. Speech Therapists, Educational Psychologists Learner and Parents consulted Revision of IEP Records of reviews by LEA
Monitoring of learner		
Assuming no or little progress is made	School requests a statutory assessment of the child Child will remain at School Action Plus until a decision has been made	School able to provide extensive information of attainment and intervention support received by the child
LEA Decision	LEA to decide if child should have a Statutory Assessment.	
Should LEA agree to an Assessment	Statutory Assessment made	Child awarded a Statement of Special Educational Needs, or child returned to School Action Plus
Annual reviews of statement or re-assessment		

Statemented children

Learners who receive a Statement of SEN will usually require a lot of support. Statutory Statements will differ in the recommendation of support which can lead to varying amounts of money being invested to meet the needs of the learner. Usually the Statement allocates a certain amount of time for one-to-one support from a teacher or a TA. However, the amount of time will vary according to the severity of need. It is the LEA that is required to fund the provisions set out in a statement.

> ... the LEA may conclude that the school could not reasonably be expected to make such provision within its own resources and that the nature of the provision suggests that the LEA should formally identify in a statement the child's needs ...
>
> (DfES 2001: 97 8:13).

Targeting and intervention

Targeting and intervention programmes are not solely designed for learners with SEN. Intervention and booster programmes such as Additional Literacy Support (ALS) and Springboard Mathematics may include learners who do not have SEN. The National Numeracy Strategy and National Literacy Strategy have developed a Wave programme, which includes interventions such as ALS. Wave intervention clearly shows how educators need to identify the needs of all learners and devise strategies to meet those needs. This process starts in Wave 1 with quality first teaching and target setting. This will affect all learners within the classroom. This stage must not be underestimated. Classroom differentiation, the strategic use of the TA, implementation of practical resources and ICT to support learning are just a few strategies that can be used to secure 'quality first teaching' within the classroom. Learners needing extra support or 'boosting' receive Wave 2 intervention programmes. These programmes are not designed to support all learners. Some may not be at the correct development stage to access these materials. Wave 3 intervention and support is support for learners with SEN. This support is specifically targeted and will mostly be individualised support that is directly linked to targets. It will form part of the IEP. For more information on wave intervention see Chapter 5.

The SENCO and Assistant SENCO

From reading the previous sections of this chapter you will have identified many duties of the SENCO. The DfES (2001: 50 5:32) summarises the main duties as:

- overseeing the day-to-day operation of the school's SEN policy
- coordinating provision for children with special educational needs
- liaising with and advising fellow teachers
- managing learning support assistants
- overseeing the records of all children with special educational needs
- liaising with parents of children with special educational needs
- contributing to the in-service training of staff
- liaising with external agencies including the LEA's support and educational psychology services, health and social services, and voluntary bodies.

The role of SENCO is demanding for one staff member and we are now seeing a new role emerging, the Assistant SENCO. A Teacher or TA may fill this role. This role may include supporting the SENCO, often in the bureaucratic duties or line management of TAs.

Specific forms of Special Educational Needs

In this section of the chapter we aim to provide you with a basic understanding of some of the commonly found SEN conditions and outline strategies that can be used to help learners.

Dyslexia

> Dyslexia is a condition that affects the ability to process language. Dyslexic learners often have difficulties in the acquisition of literacy skills, and in some cases, problems may manifest themselves in mathematics.
>
> (DfES 2001b: 2)

In the past 20 years dyslexia has been increasingly recognised as a problem for some learners and identification of it has become clearer (Miles 2004). Dyslexia mainly affects the processing skills of language. Writing skills seem to be dominated by the condition and dyslexia is probably most commonly associated with poor spelling. A learner with dyslexia may use b instead of d, mix up the letters of words in the same sentence, e.g. canker m'diggers (meaning mechanical diggers) (Pollock *et al.* 2004). Reading can also suffer, with these learners being late readers or finding difficulties with their reading fluency (Miles 2004). What is less well recognised are the difficulties related to speaking. Mispronouncing polysyllabic words or ordering problems can be linked to the condition (Pollock *et al.* 2004). Poor short term memory is also associated with dyslexia (Davis 1997). This may be seen when learners are unable to copy information accurately or transfer questions from a sheet or board onto paper. By the time they have read the information to copy and begun to write it down they have forgotten what they should be writing.

Recent research into dyslexia is revealing that this condition is due to the brain's processing skills. Scans of dyslexics' brains have shown less activity in the left side of the brain than that in non-dyslexics' (Reid 2003). The left-hand side of the brain is used more when dealing with remembering sequences, e.g. times-tables and spelling rules. It has also been noted that dyslexics suffer from left side – right side brain confusion (Miles 2004). New approaches to dyslexic teaching are constantly being produced. For example mind-mapping techniques that use a mixture of colours, pictures and a non-linear format for recording are proving successful for some. Dyslexia teaching systems have been produced and using multi-sensory teaching techniques are encouraged. Learners with dyslexia can excel with tuition adapted to their needs and through offering them strategies to cope. In addition dyslexics can possess skills and creativity in other areas such as mathematics, sciences, art and sports. Davis's (1997) book title sums this up *The Gift of Dyslexia*. In this book Davis points out that Einstein, Walt Disney, W.B. Yeats, Churchill, Cher, Edison and Jackie Stewart were or are dyslexic and claims that their genius was not in spite of their dyslexia, but because of it!

Dyscalculia

> Dyscalculia is a condition that affects the ability to acquire arithmetical skills. Dyscalculic learners may have difficulty understanding simple number concepts, lack an intuitive grasp of numbers and have problems learning number facts and procedures. Even if they produce a correct answer or use a correct method, they may do so mechanically and without confidence.
>
> (DfES 2001b: 2)

Dyscalculia is still largely unknown in England. The DfES first acknowledged the condition in 2001. Due to its short history few studies have been completed on the subject probably because its cause and definition are not clear. In schools, dyscalculia is certainly referred to as the 'numeracy side of dyslexia'. However, this is a simple definition. Unlike dyslexia there is no 'test' for dyscalculia nor do the symptoms of poor short-term memory or left side– right side brain confusion occur (Miles 2004). Nevertheless, it is a condition that can affect the learner's development in curriculum subjects and those with the condition need to be helped. In schools the SENCO should be notified of any concerns in this area.

Dyspraxia

Dyspraxia is a condition associated with movement difficulties. In the past, learners with this SEN may have been termed 'clumsy'. Like dyscalculia, dyspraxia is also a relatively new area of study. Studies into clumsy and 'motor impaired' children have been unable to identify a cause of the condition (Macintyre 2000). Many children with the condition have immature neurone development due to low birth weight or stress at birth, for example deprivation of oxygen (Macintyre 2000), although this is just one explanation. Macintyre (2000: 15) has identified the following as signs of the condition:

- Not crawling as an infant
- Reaching motor milestones late
- Difficulties in interaction
- Preference for the company of younger children
- Not sharing common interests
- Being isolated from a group
- Finding using two hands together difficult

So, what does dyspraxia mean for the learner? Dyspraxia is more than just clumsiness, and it is not simply about left-handed learners having problems with right-handed scissors (Macintyre and McVitty 2004). Dyspraxia will impact on a learner's gross motor skills, crawling, walking, running, jumping, hopping etc. Movement difficulties can affect fine motor skills too such as handwriting and cutting. Not only will this hamper general movement but also disrupt access to areas of the curriculum, PE and art for example. Social development may also be slowed down. A learner not being able to play with their peers due to not being able to 'keep up' in the playground will fall behind in socialisation skills too. Problems with self-esteem and bullying may also occur.

 Task 9E

Brian is a TA working in a high school with a male student who has a Statement for Dyspraxia. The student accesses the full curriculum and the organisation has a full inclusion policy.
Write a case study outlining the difficulties the student might face and suggest strategies that Brian could use to support the student.

Brian is a real TA. He supports the dyspraxic student in many ways. In mathematics, where he supports most, he helps the learner draw straight lines, shapes and tables by holding the ruler steady when needed. Brian makes sure that the learner's seat is near the door of the classroom (although not isolated or too far from the teacher or board), so that the he can easily get to his chair without having to go past all the tables in the classroom. Brian and the learner also leave each lesson a few minutes early so that they can arrive on time to each lesson and that they are not caught in busy corridors.

Conclusion

In this chapter we have considered some of the most common forms of special educational needs that you may encounter and we have outlined procedures for supporting these needs and reporting observations to the SENCO. We have considered how current practice within schools in relation to SEN links to the legislative framework and we have encouraged you to question the whole process of Inclusion. If you would like to read more the following section should help you.

Bibliography

Davis, R. (1997) *The Gift of Dyslexia* (2nd edn), New York: Berkley Publishing Group.
DfES (2001) *Special Educational Need Code of Practice*, London: HMSO.
DfES (2001b) *Guidance to Support Pupils with Dyslexia and Dyscalculia*, London: DfES; available: http://www.standards.dfes.gov.uk/primary/publications/mathematics/12812/nns_dyslexia051201.pdf.
DfES (2002) *Special Educational Need Revised Code of Practice*, London: HMSO.
DfES (2004) *Five-year Strategy for Children and Learners*, London: HMSO.
Education Act 1981.
Education Act 1993.
Education Reform Act 1988.
Fredrickson, N. and Cline, T. (2002) *Special Educational Needs, Inclusion and Diversity*, Maidenhead: Open University Press.
Jenkinson, J. (1997) *Mainstream or Special? Educating Students with Disabilities*, London: Routledge.
Macintyre, C. (2000) *Dyspraxia in the Early Years*, London: David Fulton.
Macintyre, C. and McVitty, K. (2004) *Movement and Learning in the Early Years: Supporting Dyspraxia (DCD) and Other Difficulties*, London: Paul Chapman Publishing.
Miles, T.R. (2004) *Dyslexia and Stress*, Philadelphia, PA: Whurr Publishers.
Ofsted (2001) *Special Educational Needs and Disability: Towards Inclusive Schools*, London: HMSO.
Ofsted (2004) *Educational Inclusion, Guidance for Inspectors and Schools*, London: HMSO.
Pollock, J., Waller, E. and Politt, R. (2004) *Day-to-day Dyslexia in the Classroom*, New York: Routledge Falmer.
Reid, G. (2003) *Dyslexia and Literacy: An Introduction to Theory and Practice*, New York: Wiley & Sons.
Special Educational Needs and Disability Act 2001 SENDA.
Soan, S. (2004) *Recent Legislation, Additional Educational Needs (AEN and Inclusion From Additional Educational Needs – Inclusive Approaches to Teaching*, London: David Fulton.
Warnock, Baroness (Chair) (1978) *Special Educational Needs: Report of the Committee of Enquiry into the Education of Handicapped Children and Young People*, Cmnd. 7212, London: HMSO.

Chapter 10

Child protection

This chapter will provide you with an overview of the issues associated with child protection. We will look at the need for rigorous child protection procedures within the school and at the role of the teaching assistant in supporting the policy of the school.

Child Protection

The Children Act 1989 is the legislation which underpins child welfare and the protection of children from abuse. The Children Act 1989 gives every child the right to protection from abuse and exploitation and the right to have enquires made to safeguard his or her welfare. Sections 27 and 47 of the Act place duties on a number of agencies to assist social services departments acting on behalf of children and young people in need for enquiring into allegations of child abuse. Circular 10/95 sets out the responsibilities of Local Authorities, schools and teachers in protecting children from abuse and neglect. The key points are that:

- The school must have a child protection policy and a designated person to liaise with statutory agencies.
- The policy must include procedures for handling suspected cases of the abuse of pupils, including procedures to be followed should a member of staff be accused of abuse.
- All staff should know the designated person, be familiar with the procedures and be alert to any signs of potential abuse.
- No one should personally investigate cases of alleged or suspected abuse but should pass their concerns on to the designated person.
- No one should guarantee confidentiality to a pupil.
- The person who notices the abuse should make a record which includes the time, date, place and people who were present as well as what was said. This record may be used in any subsequent court proceedings.

An important part of child protection is for employers to have appropriate procedures when appointing staff. This will include a check to identify the possible criminal background of people who will have substantial unsupervised access to children and a check with the Department for Education and Employment's *List 99*. This is a list of people who have no or restricted access to children because they pose a significant risk to their safety.

Defining child abuse

Child abuse is hard to define. Whilst there are some actions that are regarded as illegal, such as physically beating a child and are therefore are easy to define as abuse, there are some actions which are situation dependent such as emotional abuse. We can identify four main categories of abuse:

 Physical
 Emotional
 Sexual
 Neglect

In order to be registered on a local authority child abuse register a child has to be defined as suffering from or at risk of suffering from significant harm in one of these four areas. The key skill is to recognise the signs of abuse, respond appropriately and to know when and how to report suspicions of abuse.

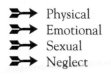

Task 10A

Think about examples of behaviour that may indicate that a child is being abused.

The clearest indication that abuse is taking place is a change in behaviour. The abused child may become withdrawn, or unusually aggressive. It is important to realise, however, that these characteristics do not always mean that a child is being abused. Abuse is difficult to detect. With long term abuse it is easy to view changes in behaviour as part of the child's developing disposition.

Physical abuse can often be identified through injuries which may be observed during PE sessions. Again the presence of a bruise or two does not necessarily mean abuse is taking place but all staff need to be alerted to the possibility. Recurrent or extensive injuries may be indicators of physical abuse. Physical abuse may involve shaking, throwing, poisoning, hitting, burning or scalding, suffocating, drowning or otherwise causing physical harm to a child. There are some common sites of non-accidental injury. Injuries here should always be queried. They include ears, bruising to eyes, nose, injuries to the mouth, thumbprints on shoulders, upper arms, inner arms, chest, back, buttocks, stomach and thighs.

Sexual abuse involves forcing or enticing a child to take part in sexual activities, whether or not they are aware of what is happening. Sexual abuse is extremely difficult to detect. It may be indicated by a sudden change in behaviour, the presence of a sexually transmitted disease, or by pregnancy.

Emotional abuse is persistent emotional ill-treatment resulting in severe and persistent adverse effects on a child's emotional development. It is often achieved by making the individual feel worthless, inadequate, or conditionally valued. Again emotional abuse is very difficult to detect. There may be behavioural changes such as changes in weight and self-harm.

Neglect is the ongoing failure to meet a child's basic physical and/or psychological needs resulting in extreme cases in serious impairment of health or development. Neglect can be identified when individuals demonstrate signs of constant hunger, poor personal hygiene, inadequate clothing, tiredness or untreated medical complaints.

There are some further categories of abuse that should be acknowledged.

Child pornography involves the taking of sexually explicit photographic or video images of children. Such images may be for personal use or may be distributed. The ability to digitally enhance and modify images has meant greater risk for children and a concern over the taking of photographs and videos within the school. Taking photographs of children in school is not illegal but there may be legal requirements or individual school or LA policy requirements that prevent you from photographing pupils. Many schools now regard photographs of pupils and staff as personal data under the terms of the Data Protection Act 1998. Using photographs therefore requires the consent of either the individual concerned or in the case of pupils, their legal guardians. Many schools do use photographs for publicity purposes but adopt good practice such as not naming the pupil if the photograph is used or not using a photograph when a pupil is named.

Child prostitution is the involvement of children in commercial sexual exploitation.

Domestic violence may be in the form of physical or emotional abuse or a combination of both. Children may suffer during episodes of violence and witnessing the physical and emotional suffering of a parent can cause distress. Domestic violence can impact upon the ability of the adult victims to provide effective parenting. Signs of a child suffering as a result of domestic violence can include serious anxiety and distress. School may be the safe retreat from problems at home or children may avoid school in order to remain on the home to protect the parent or younger siblings. Domestic violence can affect health, educational attainment and emotional well-being and development. Children witnessing domestic violence can exhibit behavioural difficulties, absenteeism, ill health, bullying, anti-social behaviour and substance abuse. Section 120 of the Adoption and Children Act 2002, updates the definition of 'harm' in the Children Act 1989 s.31(9) by adding that seeing the 'impairment suffered from seeing or hearing the ill-treatment of another' may cause harm. This has the effect of strengthening the case for significant harm through domestic violence, or the abuse of another in the household.

Forced marriage is an abuse of human rights and falls within the Crown Prosecution Service definition of domestic violence. Young people at risk of a forced marriage exhibit symptoms of emotional and/or physical abuse. Many professionals feel that this is a private and cultural family matter. However, this anxiety is unnecessary as no culture or religion sanctions forced marriage. A forced marriage is different to an arranged marriage where parties consent of their own free will.

Female genital mutilation refers to all procedures which involve partial or total removal of the external female genitalia or injury to the female genital organs for cultural or any other reason. Depending on the degree of mutilation there can be serious health implications including severe pain and shock, infection, urinary tract problems, haemorrhage and injury to adjacent tissues. Long term implications can involve damage of the external reproductive system and severe uterine, vaginal and pelvic infections. There may be complications in menstruation, pregnancy and childbirth and psychological damage. The Female Genital Mutilation Act 2004 makes it an offence for UK nationals or permanent UK residents to carry out female genital mutilation even in countries where the practice is legal. To reflect the serious harm that this mutilation causes, the Act lays down a maximum penalty of 14 years' imprisonment.

Fabrication of illness refers to the fabrication or induction of illness in a child. There are three main ways of a parent or carer fabricating or inducing illness in a child which are not mutually exclusive. The parent/carer may fabricate the signs and symptoms of illness including inventing a past medical history. The parent/carer may fabricate signs and symptoms by falsifying records, letters, documents and specimens of bodily fluids. Additionally, the parent/carer may induce illness using a variety of means. In most cases children are found to have been subjected to a combination of abuses.

The concept of **significant harm** was introduced with the Children Act 1989 as the threshold used to justify the compulsory intervention in family life in the interests of the child. The local authority is under a duty to investigate where it has reasonable cause to suspect that a child is suffering, or likely to suffer significant harm (s.47). A court may only make a care order (committing the child to the care of the local authority) or supervision order (putting the child under the supervision of a social worker, or a probation officer) if it is satisfied that the child is suffering, or is likely to suffer, significant harm; and that the harm or likelihood of harm is attributable to a lack of adequate parental care or control (Section 31 of the Children Act 1989). There are no absolute criteria upon which to rely when judging what constitutes significant harm. The court must consider the family context; the child's development within the context of their family and the wider social and cultural environment; any special needs such as a medical condition, communication difficulty or disability that may affect the child's development and care within the family; the nature of harm in terms of ill-treatment or failure to provide adequate care; the impact on the child's health and development; and the adequacy of parental care.

Child protection register

Each Social Services Department holds a register listing children in the area who have been identified at a child protection conference, as being at continuing risk of significant harm and hence in need of a child protection plan and registration. Schools should monitor pupils whose names are on the child protection register in line with what has been agreed in the child protection plan. The plan sets out the role of the child's parents/carers and various agencies in protecting the child. For schools this might include alerting the social worker or the Education Welfare Officer to signs which suggest changes in home circumstances or when the pupil is absent. Where a child on the protection register changes schools it is crucial that the school the child is leaving transfers the information to the receiving school immediately and informs social services.

Task 10B

Consider the following scenario.:

How would you respond in this situation?

Sam is always well behaved but he can be very quiet and does not like mixing with other children. He is reluctant to talk to adults but has built a relationship with the small group that he works with. You are the Teaching Assistant who supports that group. At the end of the school day his grandfather comes to collect him. Sam begins to cry and shake violently and says he does not want to go home with Grandad.

Responding to Allegations and Signs of Abuse

Care must be taken in asking, and interpreting children's responses to questions about indications of abuse. The same considerations apply when a child makes an accusation of abuse or volunteers information which amounts to that. It is important to be aware of the impact that adults can have and the impact that the ways in which they talk to a child can affect both the evidence that is volunteered and the way in which this is viewed should there be any subsequent criminal proceedings. Care must be taken to avoid leading questions as this can later be interpreted as putting ideas into the child's mind. For example it is better to say `tell me what happened' rather than 'did they do x to you?' It is equally important not to panic and jump to conclusions. There may be an innocent explanation for any worrying behaviour witnessed and you should discuss your concerns with the designated member of staff who is trained for this purpose and will follow up any concerns. Thus care should be taken to interpret correctly apparent signs of abuse and neglect. Reporting procedures for all pupils are exactly the same. Learners who have difficulties in communicating should be given the chance to express themselves to a member of staff with appropriate communication skills.

Physical contact may be a necessary part of teaching some pupils with SEN, for example visually impaired children or those with profound and multiple learning difficulties. Many teachers and teaching assistants are worried about physical contact with pupils because of the connection between physical contact and child protection. The legislation on discipline and child protection does not make it illegal for you simply to touch a pupil. Circular 10/95 makes it clear that it is unnecessary and unrealistic to suggest that teachers should touch pupils only in emergencies. Physical contact with younger pupils is inevitable as you may need to reassure and support them. Nevertheless, it is sensible to remember that even perfectly innocent actions can sometimes be misconstrued and you should be careful to avoid touching pupils on any part of the body where the action may be misconstrued. Moreover, some pupils may find any physical contact distressing. It is widely recognised as good practice that any member of staff should avoid being alone with a pupil in confined and secluded areas.

Advice for children

It is important that children are given clear advice and guidance on managing abusive situations. This can be done through the coverage of child abuse in the PSHE curriculum.

There are several key messages that children need to receive. If someone is hurting them it is not their fault. They are not alone and there are people who can help them and stop them feeling scared or hurt. Children may be frightened of the person hurting them but they need to be reassured that there are things they can do to get help. Children also need to know that it is acceptable to tell someone they trust that they or someone they know is being hurt. They should never feel embarrassed or alone or take the blame for someone hurting them. Children can be taught about the risks of different kinds of child abuse through the curriculum and be equipped with the skills they need to help them to stay safe. Teaching children ways to prevent or talk about abuse should be done sensitively. Circular 10/95 makes it clear that children should be given advice on help lines and if necessary be given access to telephones.

Bullying is deliberately hurtful behaviour, repeated over a period of time where there is an imbalance of power between the person perpetrating the bullying and the person being bullied. It can take many forms, but the three main types are physical (e.g. hitting, kicking, theft), verbal (e.g. name calling, racist remarks) or indirect (e.g spreading rumours, excluding someone from social groups). It is important for schools to have a whole-school policy against bullying and that prompt action is taken to prevent or stop bullying. Pupils should know how to let adults know there is a problem. They should also know how staff will investigate and act upon cases of bullying in the school. Bullying incidents between children would not normally be referred as cases of child abuse. For further information on bullying see Chapter 8.

What to do if you suspect abuse

All schools should have procedures for handling suspected cases of abuse of pupils, but the responsibility for investigating such cases lies with other agencies. Headteachers should have procedures in place for handling cases of suspected abuse (including allegations against teachers) which are consistent with those agreed by the local Area Child Protection Committee and easily available to all staff for reference. All schools should appoint a designated member of staff to co-ordinate action within the school and liaise with other agencies on suspected abuse cases and ensure that the designated member of staff receives appropriate training and support. Staff training should ensure that all staff are alert to signs of possible abuse and know how to report any concerns or suspicions. Schools should also make parents aware of the school's child protection policy.

Child protection procedures

Schools have an important role to play. The school can be best placed to notice the signs of abuse and they have a duty to report any concerns they have about children to the local authority social services. Where abuse is suspected or an allegation is made, teachers and other members of staff should report the information to the designated teacher who will refer the case to or discuss it with the investigating agencies according to the procedures established by the local Area Child Protection Committee and by the LA. Deciding to make a referral and deciding not to refer are serious decisions and require careful judgement.

Designated teacher

The designated teacher has a specific responsibility for the co-ordination of child protection procedures within the school and for liaison with social services and other agencies. All staff need to be made aware of who the designated teacher is as all cases of suspected abuse should be reported to him or her. The designated teacher is usually a senior member of staff who will have had appropriate training and will know how to identify the signs and symptoms of abuse and when to make a referral. They will be familiar with the local Area Child Protection Committee/LA procedures and the role and responsibilities of the investigating agencies and how to liaise with them. The designated teacher will understand the requirements of record keeping and confidentiality in relation to child protection. All schools are required to have a designated teacher. Anyone who suspects abuse should report their concerns immediately and directly to this person. When the suspected abuse has been allegedly committed by a member of staff in the school, the designated teacher should inform the headteacher. Under no circumstances should any allegation of abuse be discussed with another member of staff. If the allegation is against the headteacher then the Chair of the Governing Body should be informed and/or the Local Authority Designated officer.

The role of the Teaching Assistant

In order to comply with the school policy and procedure for child protection you need to know how to respond to a child making an allegation of abuse. If you suspect child abuse you need to ensure that you listen carefully to the child, reassuring them that they are not to blame. Do not try to investigate this yourself and never promise to keep a secret. You must explain what you are going to do about what the child has divulged and report your concerns to the designated teacher at the earliest opportunity. It is important to maintain confidentiality. One of the most difficult aspects of managing child protection is not letting your own feelings show. The abuse may be shocking and disturbing but you must remain calm and professional at all times. There is detailed guidance available to schools on the management of child protection. Schools now have a specific duty to promote and safeguard the welfare of all children under the age of 18. Closer integration between local authority social services, health and education departments will ensure more effective provision and support for abused children. The Children Bill 2004, heralded by the DfES green Paper *Every Child Matters* (2004) places emphasis on joined-up provision. Underpinning the bill is the understanding that child protection cannot be separated from policies that improve children's lives as a whole. In early years this collaborative provision is achieved through the 'Sure Start' initiative which places children's centres at the heart of the most deprived neighbourhoods. These combine health, education, family support, employment advice and childcare into one location. Multi-disciplinary teams work together to respond quickly to the needs of the community and to respond to the concerns of teachers and other professionals.

Conclusion

Dealing with issues of child protection is not easy. Great care must be taken to ensure that the correct policies and procedures are followed and that children are supported appropriately. Teaching Assistants should make themselves aware of the issues surrounding child protection and remain vigilant in the classroom. There is considerable guidance on child protection available on the internet from the government and children's charities which are a good source of developmental material. In this chapter we have explored some forms of abuse and the legislation developed to support a multi-agency approach to tackling this problem. As we have shown, schools are in a key position to identify some of these problems and have a duty to report them via the designated (and trained) member of staff. The Bibliography section will provide you with some further suggestions for obtaining information about child protection.

 Bibliography

Adoption and Children Act 2002.
Children Act 1989.
The Children Bill 2004.
Data Protection Act 1998.
Female Genital Mutilation Act 2004.
DfES (1995) Circular 10/95 *Protecting Children from Abuse: The Role of the Education Service*, London: HMSO.
DfES (2004) *Every Child Matters: Change for Children*, London: HMSO.

Chapter 11

Planning and assessment

In this chapter we will provide you with an introduction to planning, preparation and assessment. We look at the importance of planning and preparing for learning. We then move on to look at the principles of effective assessment practice and explore a range of assessment strategies and differences between them. We also consider the ways in which assessment practice can enhance learning through providing accurate relevant information about a learner's current stage of development. We move on to think about e-learning and the impact of this on classroom practice. Finally we consider the roles and responsibilities of those engaged in assessment and the role of the Teaching Assistant in supporting assessment.

What is planning?

The classroom is a very complex place and there are many considerations that need to be taken into account before we can deliver or support learning.

 Task 11A

Consider a standard science lesson. What must be considered before teaching and learning can take place?

In any form of teaching there are two key issues that need to be taken into account when planning learning experiences. Firstly we need to think about who the learners are and secondly we need to consider what their learning needs might be. It is important that all lessons are appropriate to the age and stage of development of the learner. This knowledge will influence the learning activities selected and the ways in which they are presented. So although choosing what is appropriate to teach will be related to the curriculum there are other factors that also play a part. It is important to ensure that all the learners being taught can participate and that their learning builds upon their existing skills and knowledge. To add to these planning issues it is also important to recognise that each learner progresses at a different rate and all of these individual needs must be met as well as the needs of the group as a whole. This aspect of planning becomes easier as those teaching get to know their learners and their abilities. Nevertheless, it is necessary to plan for the fact that individuals and groups will need varying levels of support at different times. This may be provided by the teacher or by the teaching assistant or by other professionals. Learners may have personal, social, emotional or behavioural needs that might affect their engagement with the lesson. It is also necessary to consider how well the learning environment meets these needs. For example, there may be some individuals who will require support away from the classroom setting. In addition the resources available need to be adjusted to meet the needs of all the learners. So when planning, it is important to think about what will be required, in what quantities and by whom. The planning should take account of any needs for specialist resources, the knowledge staff need in order for them to be used effectively and take into account any health and safety implications. As you can see planning and preparing for learning are complex activities.

Differentiation

Differentiation is the process of maximising learning for all by taking account of differences in learning style, motivation, ability and reflecting individual variation in the classroom. Differentiation is linked to the principle of equality of opportunity. All learners have the right to learn effectively. The emphasis is on what is learned not on what is taught. The confidence, motivation and individuality of the learner is important and planning should seek to maximise learning by taking account of the differences learners bring to the classroom.'Teachers should teach the knowledge, skills and understanding in ways that suit their pupils' abilities.' (QCA 1999 National Curriculum Documents)

Learning objectives

Objectives or learning outcomes for each lesson are the specific skills or knowledge and understanding that learners are expected to be able to demonstrate at the end of the lesson. Having objectives focuses attention on what is to be taught, and how we assess any individual's learning. Objectives should be a clear statement of the expected learning outcomes and are not indicators of the activities that form part of the lesson. Therefore lessons should be measurable against the stated objectives and as such they can be used as criteria for assessment. It is also possible to have differentiated learning objectives for particular learners for the same lesson.

Types of planning

There are a number of types of planning that operate within educational settings but all of the planning is interlinked. As already indicated, planning provides a structure to teaching and learning and brings together learners and curriculum to enable learning to take place. A planned programme of study is known as the formal curriculum. It is the curriculum that all educators 'plan' to cover. It sets out the intended activities for learning and defines the order in which the activities will be covered. The 'hidden curriculum' refers to the learning that takes place in everyday experiences that has not been planned for. The hidden curriculum can affect learners' attitudes to learning. The hidden curriculum is important because of its influence on attitudes to learning and on learner progress. Effective planning is based on understanding how learners learn and knowing what their prior knowledge, understanding and skills are and how this relates to the specific content, knowledge, skills and concepts of each subject within the overall structure of the curriculum. It is therefore important that all professionals working with learners in schools are aware of the appropriate National Curriculum Frameworks for teaching the Schemes of Work for the different subjects (QCA/DfES).

In schools there are three levels of planning. Long-term planning shows how the organisation will cover the curriculum. It outlines how the curriculum is structured within year groups and across Key Stages and sets out how much time is allocated to each part of the curriculum. It shows how the content is covered in terms of breadth and depth. Medium-term planning details the subject programme coverage that will be followed by a group of learners within the organisation. This will be year group- or class-specific. The purpose of a medium-term plan is to provide the detailed framework for classroom practice. It details the knowledge, skills and processes to be taught during the half-term or term and sets out the linkage to other subjects. Medium-term plans make use of the National Curriculum, the Frameworks for English and Mathematics and the DfES/QCA Schemes of Work. The medium-term plan may be linked to practical considerations such as the organisation's timetable, holiday dates, availability of resources and examinations.

   Task 11B

Look at a medium term plan. Use the following list to become familiar with the content.

Title of unit	Subject areas	Key aims
Learning objectives	Attainment targets	Resources
Level descriptions	Differentiation	Assessment

Detail of concepts, knowledge, skills and attitudes to be taught
National Curriculum programme of study
Activities showing progression, organisation and teaching methods
Learning environment modifications or usage

Short-term planning refers to weekly, daily or individual lesson plans. Short-term plans have clear learning objectives and set out the activities learners will undertake. They indicate where the lesson will be differentiated to meet the needs of learners. They outline the strategies to be used for teaching and supporting learning. Assessment strategies and an evaluation of the lesson will also be recorded on the short-term plan. Long-, medium- and short-term plans link together. The short-term plan is determined by the medium-term plan which is in turn created from the long-term plan. Planning runs in cycles, termly, yearly and sometimes operating over several years.

Teaching Assistants play a crucial role in the planning process. Knowing and understanding the learning objectives for a lesson will enable the Teaching Assistant to provide the most effective support for learning. Teaching Assistants can contribute to the assessment of the learning taking place through their observations of learners. Teachers may involve Teaching Assistants as they draw up their plans and may utilise particular knowledge TAs have about particular learners and their ideas for learning.

What is assessment?

Assessment is the way in which we gather information about what learners are able to do at the end of a lesson that they couldn't do at the start of the lesson. We choose assessment strategies that enable us and the learners to judge what they have achieved during the lesson and whether the learning objective has been achieved. Figure 11.1 shows the cyclical nature of planning and assessment and how they are interrelated.

Types of assessment

The four main forms of assessment; formative, summative, diagnostic and evaluative.

Briefly *formative* assessment is informal and ongoing; it can involve written work and celebrate positive achievement. *Summative* assessment is formal and involves record keeping, measuring what has been achieved over a given period of time at a specific point of time, e.g. National Tests (SATs). *Diagnostic* assessment uses work/observations to assess weakness, e.g. analysing misconceptions in maths by studying the working out of a learner and asking them to explain their thinking. Finally *evaluative* assessment determines the overall success of a particular initiative. These forms of assessment correspond to and provide information that assists with short-, medium- and long-term stages of planning. Formative and diagnostic assessments are linked to short-term planning and are also called 'assessment for learning'. Summative and evaluative assessment are linked to medium- and long- term planning, and are also known as 'assessment of learning'.

Figure 11.1   The cyclical nature of planning and assessment

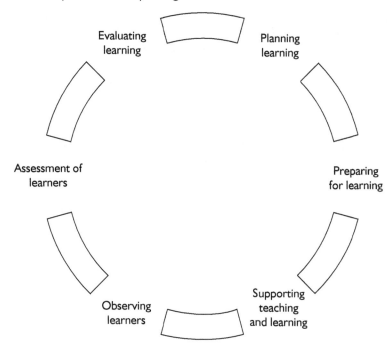

What is short-term assessment?

Short-term assessment is undertaken informally in every lesson. It provides the information that enables adjustments to be made to subsequent lessons. It is a continuous process and helps us to make judgements about learners' progress against their targets. For example in a primary school a target might be 'to recognise capital letters'. Such targets are vital in Individual Education Plans (IEPs) for learners with Special Educational Needs (SEN). During a lesson you observe that the learner can now recognise the capital letter at the start of their own name. As a result you decide not to include these capital letters in an activity scheduled for later in the week and replace them with other as yet unknown capital letters in order to expand their knowledge. This is short-term assessment. It is important that when we are marking and monitoring learners' work we provide constructive oral or written feedback that acknowledges their successes, helps them see what they need to do to improve further and sets them targets to achieve. Short-term assessment informs this process and can be recorded by writing brief evaluative comments about the learner's response to a task. It is important to record any notable or exceptional performance.

What is medium-term assessment?

Medium-term assessment reviews and records the progress that learners are making against key objectives. This process is undertaken approximately every half-term thus reviewing learners' progress towards targets over a period of time and helping to inform planning for the next half-term. Records of medium-term assessments are helpful in producing end-of-year assessments.

What is long-term assessment?

Long-term assessment for learners is important. This assessment usually takes place at the end of a year or at the end of a programme of study. It provides information about how successfully objectives have been met and how well learners are progressing. Long-term assessments are useful in helping the organisation as a whole set targets for future years. Long-term assessments can also be beneficial to a learner's next teacher and should be passed on. In addition, they are used as the basis for writing reports and reporting to parents. In England a summary of the English, mathematics and science tests and teacher assessment results must be published by each school in its prospectus and governors' annual report along with national comparative assessments for the previous year. Most long-term assessments are made using standard tests. For example in Years 2, 6 and 9 children undertake statutory tests of attainment – SATs. These results enable the DfES to monitor national and local trends in progress.

There are however critics of such measures of attainment. There are a number of issues that might affect results that make it difficult to demonstrate a school's effectiveness. For example, some schools may have a proliferation of children from educated homes. In these areas schools can expect to do well whether or not the teachers make an effort. Similarly, schools with an intake of children from a poor socio-economic background may work extremely hard and teach very effectively but their results may not be a high as othr schools in different areas. There is now a pressure to measure schools in terms of 'value added' measures. This considers how much the learners have improved during their time at the school, therefore they are measured/tested on entry. Schools may also be strong in delivering social skills and a positive environment but not be strong on test results. This is a whole area of debate that you need to think about. You must consider how you feel about tests and whether they are true measures of a school or its learners.

Foundation Stage assessment

The Foundation Stage Profile is the statutory assessment for children in the final year of the Foundation Stage. It is completed for each child during the second half of the summer term, and summarises each child's progress and learning needs in relation to the Early Learning Goals at the end of the Foundation Stage.

Statutory National Curriculum Tests

There is a statutory requirement to assess children formally at the end of Key Stage 1 (KS1) Year 2 age 7 in English and Mathematics, KS 2 Year 6 age 11 in English, mathematics and science and KS 3 Year 9 age 14 in English, mathematics and science. NC tests and tasks are provided by the Qualifications and Curriculum Authority (QCA) and undertaken by learners in these year groups in May of each year. The tests are designed to help teachers assess learners' strengths and weaknesses and determine what they understand about a subject. As well as standard versions of the key stage tests, QCA produces modified versions for learners with visual impairment. QCA publishes non-statutory tests in English and Mathematics for Years 3, 4, 5, 7 and 8. Most schools use these to track children's progress year by year. QCA also produces optional assessment tasks for learners working above and below the level of the tests.

In addition to national testing in Years 2 and 6, teacher assessment of each learner's progress is required. Assessments are made against the level descriptions in the National Curriculum. Teachers use their knowledge of a learner's work to judge which level description best fits their performance across different contexts. Up-to-date records are kept of each learner's attainment along with samples of the children's work as evidence of attainment.

Assessing learning

There are a variety of methods to assess learning. These include:

- noting a learner's reactions to learning tasks
- discussion
- questioning
- using assessment tasks
- using tests
- observation

Observation is important. A learner who is not fully engaged in the task may be struggling because the work is too difficult or bored because it is too easy.

The National Curriculum level descriptors, the National Literacy and Numeracy Strategy Framework for teaching from Reception to Year 6 provide an indication of the level of achievement expected for children in Key Stages 1–3. Each GCSE Syllabus provides information on levels of achievement expected in Key Stage 4. In post-16 education the levels of achievement are detailed in curriculum syllabus documentation.

Assessment of learning

Assessment of learning is the summative and evaluative assessment that ascertains the level a learner has reached. Such assessments can be conducted termly, annually or at the end of a key stage. Assessment of learning is the measurement of what learners can do and is used to improve learning. Assessment for learning is the ongoing day-to-day formative and diagnostic assessment that takes place to gather information on what a learner can or cannot do and how future lessons will need to be adapted to account for this.

> Assessment for learning is the process of seeking and interpreting evidence for use by learners and their teachers to decide where the learners are in their learning, where they need to go and how best to get there.
>
> (Assessment Reform Group 2002)

Assessment for learning is a collaborative process in which teachers share learning targets with learners who then know and recognise the standards required of them. In this process there is feedback that leads learners to identify what they should do next in order to improve. It is underpinned by the assumption that every learner can improve their performance and that reviewing and reflecting upon performance and progress with teachers are essential to the learning process. This assessment becomes 'formative assessment' when the evidence is used to adapt the teaching work to meet learning needs. It thus informs the planning process. As a consequence of involving the learner in the process this form of assessment should be sensitive and constructive taking account of the emotional impact on the learner. We should be aware of the impact that comments, marks and grades can have on learners' confidence and enthusiasm and should be as constructive as possible in the feedback that is given. Comments that focus on the work rather than the person are more constructive for both learning and motivation. It is also important to take account of the importance of learner motivation and develop the learners' capacity for self-assessment. Assessment for learning is central to effective classroom practice and is a key professional skill for all adults working with learners in all contexts.

Characteristics of assessment for learning

Assessment for learning is based upon the idea that learners improve most if they understand the aim of their own learning, where they are in relation to this aim and how they can achieve it. Sharing learning goals with learners is important as it enables them to know and recognise the standards they need to aim for. Information on how to improve is crucial to any individual and success is underpinned by the belief that every learner can improve. Such assessment is collaborative with both teacher and learner reviewing and reflecting on performance and progress. It is also developmental in that it encourages learners' self-assessment techniques. Being part of the review process raises standards and empowers learners. Key characteristics of assessment for learning are the use of effective questioning techniques, diagnostic marking and feedback strategies, shared learning goals and peer- and self-assessment.

A teacher's planning should provide opportunities for both learner and teacher to obtain and use information about progress towards learning goals. It also has to be flexible enough to respond to initial and emerging ideas and skills. Planning should include strategies to ensure that learners understand the goals they are pursuing and the criteria that will be applied in assessing their work, how learners will receive feedback, how they will take part in assessing their learning and how they will be helped to make further progress. Learners should become as aware of the 'how' of their learning as they are of the 'what'. Much of what teachers and learners do in classrooms can be described as assessment, that is, tasks and questions prompt learners to demonstrate their knowledge, understanding and skills. What learners say and do are then observed and interpreted, and judgements are made about how learning can be improved. As a consequence assessment for learning should be regarded as a key professional skill for teachers and TAs. Both require the professional knowledge and skills to plan for assessment; observe learning; analyse and interpret evidence of learning; give feedback to learners; and support learners in self-assessment. Teachers and TAs should be supported in developing these skills through initial and continuing professional development.

It is important to emphasise progress and achievement rather than failure. Comparison with others who have been more successful is unlikely to motivate learners. It can also lead to their withdrawing from the learning process in areas where they have been made to feel they are 'no good'. Motivation can be preserved and enhanced by assessment methods that protect the learner's autonomy, provide some choice and constructive feedback, and create opportunity for self-direction. Understanding and commitment follow when learners have some part in deciding goals and identifying criteria for assessing progress. Communicating assessment criteria involves discussing them with learners using terms that they can understand, providing examples of how the criteria can be met in practice and engaging learners in peer- and self-assessment. Learners should receive constructive guidance about how to improve. In order to ensure this teachers need to:

- Pinpoint the learner's strengths and advise them how to develop them.
- Be clear and constructive about any weaknesses and how they might be addressed.
- Provide opportunities for learners to improve upon their work.

Independent learners have the ability to seek out and gain new skills, new knowledge and new understandings. Assessment for learning should recognise the full range of achievements of all learners and should be used to enhance all learners' opportunities to learn in all areas of educational activity. It should enable all learners to achieve their best and to have their efforts recognised. This process is effective and improves achievement where learners show changes in their attitudes to learning and in their motivation, self-esteem, independence, initiative and confidence. This may mean that they demonstrate changes in their responses to questions, in contributions to class discussions and in explanations and descriptions. It is important that educators know their learners well understanding why they might make a mistake and be able to make judgements about next steps or interventions. It is also necessary to provide examples of a variety of skills, attitudes, standards and qualities to aim towards. So learners need to be encouraged to take responsibility for their learning by providing opportunities for them to describe their response to learning, the strategies they have used or are using and the judgements they make in relation to their progress.

Methods of assessing learners

We can use a variety of methods to assess learning. Questioning is one of the key skills professionals utilise when assessing learning. We can analyse responses to questions and the questions that learners ask, in order to find out what they know, understand and can do. We can use questions diagnostically to find out what the learners' specific misconceptions are in order to target teaching more effectively. Some questions are better than others at providing assessment opportunities. Often the way a question is phrased can make a significant difference to the thought processes and language demands learners need to go through and the extent to which learners reveal their understanding.

Task 11C

Consider these two questions.

1) Is 3 a prime number?
2) Why is 3 an example of a prime number?

Which question is better at enabling an assessment to take place?

If we ask 'Is 3 a prime number?' we are likely to get a yes / no response which could be a guess. We cannot assess what the learner knows. If we use the question 'Why is 3 an example of a prime number?' we can help the learner recall their knowledge of the properties of prime numbers and the properties of 3 and compare them. This could result in an answer which states what a prime number is – a number with two factors and linking this to the knowledge that the number 3 has two factors – 1 and 3. This question places greater demand upon the learner and a higher degree of articulation. The learner needs to explain and justify their thought processes.

Task 11D

Think of other types of questions that are effective in providing assessment opportunities.

Some examples of questions that are effective in providing assessment opportunities are:

➤➤ How can we be sure that...?
➤➤ Is it ever/always true/false that...?
➤➤ How would you explain...?
➤➤ What does that tell us about...?

Marking and feedback strategies are essential elements in helping learners improve. Comments that are not related to the learning intention or task are unhelpful when using assessment for learning. It is much better to give feedback which helps learners improve in the specific activity as this will help to close the learning gap. It is important to establish trust before giving feedback. Group and plenary sessions are effective as forums for providing feedback as they allow learners to evaluate for themselves where they have made mistakes and what they need to do to improve.

Giving feedback involves making time to talk to and teaching learners to become reflective about their work in relation to the learning objectives. It therefore requires careful planning. Feedback is more effective if it is given while still relevant and is most effective when it confirms that learners are on the right track and stimulates correction or improvement. It is a way of 'scaffolding' learning, working best when learners are not given complete solutions as soon as they experience difficulty but are helped to find alternative solutions. Feedback on progress over a number of attempts is more effective than feedback on one attempt treated in isolation. Shared dialogue is important and oral feedback is more effective than written feedback. Learners need to have the skills to ask for help and the ethos of the organisation should encourage them to do so. A culture of success should be promoted in which every learner achieves by building on personal previous performance.

Learning is more effective when the learning goals are shared. Planning sets out the learning objectives for a lesson. The learning objective relates to what the learner will learn and not the task they will undertake. Assessment criteria or learning outcomes are often written in formal language that learners may not understand. It is important to explain clearly the reasons for the lesson or activity in terms of the learning objectives and share the specific assessment criteria with learners. When giving feedback we can help learners to understand what they have done well and what they need to develop in relation to the specific learning objective. Peer- and self-assessment can be useful tools to engage learners in their own learning process. If learners know what they need to learn and why and can assess their understanding, gaps in their own knowledge and areas they need to work on, they will achieve more than if they sit passively in a classroom. Peer-assessment can be effective because learners can clarify their own ideas and understanding of the learning intention and the assessment criteria while marking another learner's work. It must be managed carefully and sensitively. It should never be used to compare performance as it will demotivate learners. Learners who reflect on their own work can be supported to admit problems without a risk to their self-esteem and can be given time to work problems out.

Assessment in the National Curriculum

In schools, assessment of learning is governed by legislation. Details of the legislation covering the setting and publication of targets can be accessed from the internet. References are included at the end of this chapter. It is also important to be aware of the Data Protection Act 1998 which covers the responsibilities of organisations in relation to the gathering and storage of personal data. This states that information should be obtained fairly and kept only as long as necessary. It should be relevant to requirements and not used in any way that is not compatible with its purpose. The Children Act 1989 also requires that children's welfare is put first and that children should be consulted and informed about what is to happen to them. Personal information kept by schools should only be accessible to adults who need it.

Roles and responsibilities

Within an organisation there will be several people involved in assessment. There will be an assessment policy to ensure consistency. The policy will also be a statement of the aims and intentions of the organisation in relation to assessment practice. It will state the aims and objectives of assessment, ways of managing the assessment process, roles and responsibilities and mechanisms for recording and reporting. In schools the governing body and the headteacher have a responsibility to collect information about learners' progress in national tests and assessments. Most organisations devolve the management of assessment to a subject leader. The assessment of learners who have special educational needs will be maintained centrally by the SENCO and may be passed to outside agencies. Subject leaders will keep records from assessments within their subject area for the whole organisation. Most importantly, teachers and teaching staff will be involved in the day-to-day collection and management of assessment for their learners. The teaching assistant will participate in all aspects of assessment. Some of this will be assessment of learning. Much of it will be assessment for learning. Much of this assessment is informal but essential to enable the teacher to plan for the next stage of learning. The key to providing effective support for assessment in the classroom is to remember to respond to the learner in relation to shared learning intention, indicating successes and what and where to improve.

E-assessment

E-learning systems can offer a different form of assessment through enabling the teacher to conduct a process of data analysis and the learner to access interactive feedback. Learners can receive personalised support through systems that offer 'assessment for learning'. E-learning also provides the means to assess the new kinds of related skills needed for life and work in the knowledge economy. By aligning assessment and using ICT effectively and efficiently, e-learning can contribute to raising standards and improving the quality of teaching and learning within the organisation. It can be argued that e-learning and e-assessment removes barriers to achievement and help widen participation, giving people the skills to prepare them for success in the workplace. E-assessment can be formative, diagnostic and adaptive. It can also be used for summative assessment – assessment of learning. Online assessment has the potential to overcome barriers such as time, location and cost. 'On demand' testing can enable learners who lack confidence to become more motivated, as they are able to progress at their own pace and demonstrate knowledge specific to their interests or to a task in the workplace. Each curriculum subject has differing requirements and may benefit from interactive or online assessment in a variety of ways.

Conclusion

In this chapter we have explored the relationship between planning and assessment. We have seen the importance of assessment for learning within the planning cycle and the effects this approach might have on learners. We have also considered effective strategies for involving learners in their own assessment process and have outlined the legislative and curriculum requirements underpinning teaching and learning. The importance of the educator in the process of developing the learners' ability to reflect on their own learning has been stressed and we have suggested some strategies for drawing learners into this process.

If you are interested and would like to read more use the B[...]
for further investigation.

 Bibliography

Assessment Reform Group (2002a) *Principles of Assessment fo[...]*
    Practice, Cambridge: School of Education, University of Can[...]
Assessment Reform Group (2002b) *Testing, Motivation and Le[...]*
    Education, University of Cambridge.
Children Act 1989.
Data Protection Act 1998.
Education Act 1997 (See section 19 for the setting and publication of targets).
QCA (1999) *National Curriculum Documents*, http://www.qca.org.uk/14-19/11-16-schools/
    downloads/AltProvisionAtKS4-Appendix-H.pdf.

Teaching Assistant and concepts in education

In this chapter we will round off the book by providing you with an overview of some key concepts in education. Therefore we will explore some of the many questions concerning the aims and values of education and the relationship of these aims and values to society. This will deepen your understanding and awareness of how those issues affect the education of children and young people. We hope to encourage you to question educational processes in a wide variety of contexts, including your own, through an exploration of the relationship between policy and practice.

Aims in education

Task 12A

What do think of as important aims of education?
Makes notes about what you think.
What role can a teaching assistant play in assisting your organisation towards meeting these aims?

In addressing this question you may have recorded some of the following ideas. You may think that education should work in collaboration with families and the local community. You possibly think that the curriculum should aim to provide opportunities for all pupils to learn and to achieve; that the school should aim to promote pupils' spiritual, moral, social and cultural development; and prepare all pupils for the opportunities and experiences of life. You may feel that the aim of education is to raise standards of attainment and achievement for all pupils. Your personal beliefs about the aims of education will influence how you act as a Teaching Assistant. This is true of all those working as educators. They will all hold underlying beliefs that mean they act in particular ways to support these aims. Likewise when they are asked to do things which conflict with these basic beliefs they find this difficult and uncomfortable. But let us take a step back and think about where these educational aims come from.

Education and society

People develop a lot of their beliefs through their experiences of childhood. As we discussed in Chapter 2 our families, the society in which we live and the educational experiences we have all play a part in shaping the way we think and the values we hold dear. In addition, socio-economic status, social mobility and social psychology all have an impact. As educators, knowing this gives us insights into the perspectives of learners.

> The more we discover, the more we know about what pupils bring with them into the classroom and take away with them to their homes. What they bring is a groundbed of attitudes, beliefs and convictions on which the seeds of knowledge sit, take root or are quickly washed away.
>
> (MacBeath 1999: 13)

The culture in which people find themselves will also affect the value they place upon education and the way they interact with educational organisations. This includes what happens outside the formal process of education. There have been enormous changes in society over time and if we consider the last 25 years educational establishments have had to adapt to many changes such as a greater variety and number of different family arrangements, greater geographic mobility and a lack of job security to name but a few. As educators we have had to adapt educational settings to cope with this changing face of society.

Ideology and culture

Educational leaders need to create a sense of direction and purpose for their organisations in order that the people working and learning within them have a sense of what it is to be part of their establishment and how the future might be developed and created. This has involved educational leaders in developing a 'vision'. Research by Hillman and Stoll (1994a) suggested that vision is important because it expresses a direction for the organisation that is grounded in local circumstances. In other words the vision takes account of local contexts whilst looking towards the future. Consequently, in an ideal world the vision is always a step ahead of the reality and is dynamic. It can be argued, however, that in reality, developments in education tend to follow behind changes in society. Have a look at the schools represented in Figure 12.1.

In terms of the diagram, two schools (A and B) could be at different points in relation to how far they are 'in tune' with the demands of the social and economic environment. School A is 'up with the pace' and School B has 'fallen behind'. We might look at this in terms of learners' ICT and social skills. The latter are sometimes referred to as 'soft skills'. Economic changes we are already experiencing (and which are likely to become more pronounced) mean that ICT and 'soft skills' are highly prized by employers. This is evidenced by the high proportion of employers who use psychometric tests in their recruitment procedures. We might think of School A as being highly committed to developing these skills whilst School B is not. So whilst School A needs to think about how the demands on learners will change further over the next five years, School B has to consider how it is going to 'catch up' with the position that School A has already reached. It is also worth considering whether each school is likely to remain stable in this position or whether positions change and fluctuate

Figure 12.1 Strategic drift and economic and social change

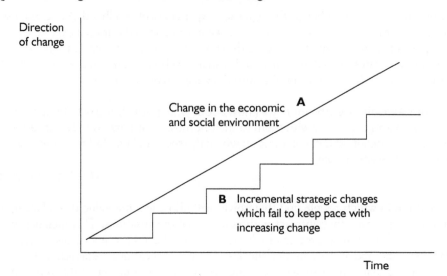

over time. Also think about whether it is reasonable to expect schools to be thinking ahead of society in general or whether they are always likely to 'lag behind'.

When considering the vision in your own organisation you need to consider whether it encompasses the values of the organisation, a view of the future context of the organisation and whether it has a distinctive view of how your organisation 'makes a difference'. This involves having high expectations of staff and learners, a commitment to inclusive practice and a focus on the learners' personal development. In addition everyone who is part of the organisation should feel involved and part of the vision.

Task 12B

What is the vision for your organisation?
How well is it communicated?

Globalisation

The term 'knowledge economy' is used to signify the employment sector 'encompassing the exploitation and use of knowledge in all production and service activities' (DTI 1999). New Labour has had a significant influence on education today and in particular have they have placed a great emphasis on the importance of the 'stakeholder'. Castells (1998) talks about the concept of 'informational capitalism', where leading business sectors have accessed higher levels of education to the point where they can re-programme themselves for the endlessly changing tasks of the production process' (Castells 1998: 341).

In this way education is expected to provide a flexible workforce. In addition, people like Bottery (2004) point out the responsibility that educators have in thinking about the globalisation of every aspect of life and in preparing learners for this. ICT is a good example of increased globalisation giving us access to world-wide communication and a potentially unlimited access to knowledge. However it is worth noting that access to ICT can be determined by social class and economics. The 'knowledge economy' is a global phenomenon. Britain has always been subject, economically and politically, to the forces of globalisation. Nation states now have a reduced capacity to control the flows of capital across their borders as trans-national companies have strengthened. Halsey *et al.* (1997) sum up the consequences of this as follows:

> Trans-national companies will invest in those nations where tax regimes and labour costs are low, while providing the infrastructure of a highly skilled workforce, sophisticated transport and financial communications. In effect, the state has to provide the conditions where a sophisticated infrastructure is delivered, while controlling tax demands and the costs of social production.
>
> (Halsey *et al.* 1997: 6)

In order to secure economic growth and prosperity New Labour have embraced globalisation.

> Globalisation is changing the nature of the nation state as power becomes more diffuse and borders more porous. Technological change is reducing the capacity of government to control a domestic economy free from external influence. The role of government in this world of change is to represent a national interest, to create a competitive base of physical infrastructure and human skills. The challenge ... is to educate and retrain for the next technologies, to prepare our country for new global competition, and to make our country a competitive base from which to produce the goods and services people want to buy.
>
> (Blair 1995: 20)

Not only does Blair see the need for education systems to meet the need of globalisation but the OECD has also identified the role of schools as laying the foundation for lifelong learning. The 'knowledge society' no longer demands employees for routine unskilled jobs. Multi-skilling and flexibility are at a premium. This view of society moves distinctly away from notions of equality to one where the fundamental divisions in knowledge are to be exploited for the greater good of the state.

> Whenever educational systems have been tempted to follow fashionable utopias that seek to break with [the] ... filtering mechanisms that are founded in a form of individual competition, the experiments have failed: education has disconnected itself both from the business world and, more generally, from our societies, which do not work that way.
>
> (European Commission 1999)

Alongside the view of an increasingly globalised society and a need to educate people to fit into a more diffuse world, there is also a push for a more cohesive society. Educational policy-making is increasingly being modelled on perceived good practice from other countries; for example, The National Literacy Strategy has many features in common with the system for literacy instruction used in Western Australian schools – the 'First Steps' approach. Policy makers are often in danger of implementing policies on the basis that it works elsewhere, without considering local variations which might in fact mean that such policies will not operate as expected. Thus, whilst some initiatives may be of a more global nature, their effects may vary widely in differing socio-geographical contexts. This creates a complex environment within which educators and the organisations within which they work have to operate, plan and teach. There are no easy answers and educational institutions face a complex array of moral dilemmas and choices. On the one hand they are told that they need to meet national targets and on the other find that individual nuances make some initiatives hard to achieve without adaptation. Teachers are known for their ability to adapt central initiatives and the way in which they are implemented to meet the needs of their own learners.

Having begun to explore some of the complexity of the educational challenge we will now consider some issues that can affect the individual's capacity to engage with learning.

Gender, ethnicity and race

Gender, ethnicity and race may impact upon the educational achievement and attainment of learners. Whilst discrimination on the basis of race, ethnicity and/or gender is prohibited, such discrimination may exist within organisations and it can also have a negative impact on our educational opportunities. Let us look at these issues individually.

Gender in education

In the last 50 years, the UK labour market has changed dramatically with women now accounting for nearly half of the workforce. There are around 17·5 million women of working age in the UK, compared to 8·6 million men of working age (ESRC 2003). Nevertheless, projections show that the trend towards more women in the workplace is set to continue and expand. Although more women are returning to work they still carry responsibility for childcare and spend more time than males on domestic chores. Moreover, women are more likely than men to work part-time and flexible hours. The employment rate for women with children is lower than those without and of those in employment, more than two-fifths of these are part-time. Women are less likely to choose self-employment and account for only one-third of new business start ups. Although women make up almost half the labour force, they are found working in a relatively narrow range of occupations. For example, women are overrepresented in the caring occupations such as nursing, education and social care. Such job 'segregation' affects males as well as females. The majority of students taking engineering apprenticeships are men, whereas the majority of apprentices in the childcare sector are women. It is important that all learners are given the opportunity to fulfil their potential irrespective of their gender. Stereotyping can be self-fulfilling with men perhaps not wanting to work with young children and women avoiding work in construction industries. Some have argued that this is based on innate abilities which are different for men and women. The 'nature verses nurture' debate is long-standing and complex.

Inequalities in work patterns are also reflected in difference between men's and women's salaries. Girls get less pocket money than boys but even as graduates women can expect to be paid 15 per cent less than men. In 1975 the Equal Pay Act was introduced to stop pay discrimination between men and women. Since 1975 the pay gap has reduced from 30 per cent to 18 per cent. For minority ethnic women however, the problem is more acute. Indian women still face a pay gap of almost 27 per cent. The pay gap is the average difference in earnings between men and women. That means that for every £1 that a man earns on average per hour, a woman earns 82 pence. The pay gap is exacerbated for women working part-time and for older female workers and there are also regional variations. The pay gap is not specific to the UK. In the USA the pay gap is 28 per cent.

There are some aspects of the patterns of women's work that have been used to explain the reasons for the pay gap. For example, women tend to commute less distance than men, restricting the employment opportunities available to them which may be associated with their childcare and domestic responsibilities. Women may also be discriminated against by employers through covert forms of discrimination such as the pay scales attached to particular jobs. The jobs attracting higher pay tend to be those traditionally associated with male employees. These higher-paid jobs have changed as male employment patterns have changed. For example, at one time the role of secretary was a highly paid professional job populated by male employees. As women moved into the role it became down-graded in pay and in status.

Task 12C

Can you think of situations where males and females are treated differently within education? What could be done to address this?

There are, for example, school situations where boys and girls line up separately. Is this justifiable? Science may be taught using language that puts girls off but encourages boys. Girls use space differently to boys. How might these issues be addressed? Education cannot directly tackle the pay gap but they can ensure that all learners understand the impact of the subject choices they make and the range of potential careers available to them. Acting as role models, all adults can encourage learners to engage with non-stereotypical subjects by making taught courses engaging for both sexes. It is an interesting fact that most celebrity chefs are male and yet food technology courses are predominantly taken by girls although there is evidence that trends are changing given the publicity people like Jamie Oliver have achieved.

Sex discrimination

The Sex Discrimination Act 1975 states that it is unlawful to discriminate against a person on the grounds of their gender. Discrimination means less favourable treatment, and there are two kinds of discrimination. First, when a person of one sex is treated less favourably, because of their sex, than another person of the opposite sex. This is direct discrimination. Second, when a condition or requirement is applied to both sexes, but the majority of one sex is not able to comply with it or where the requirement cannot be justified regardless of sex and a person is disadvantaged as a result. This is indirect discrimination.

Application of the Act in schools

In relation to schools, the Sex Discrimination Act sets out the kinds of treatment that could be regarded as discriminatory. The Act sets out guidelines, which if they are followed, should ensure that the organisation complies with the legislation. It is unlawful to discriminate against a person on the grounds of gender by refusing an application for admission to the school or by using a separate language in any school paperwork; by refusing access to any benefits, facilities or services which are open to the opposite sex and by subjecting them to any other detriment. In addition, both genders must have precisely the same access to the curriculum. A good curriculum is therefore relevant to all learners; it reflects diversity and cultural heritage and it builds in positive images and positive action to ensure equality of opportunity is met. Similarly, the whole environment should be conducive to ensuring equal opportunity.

Both written and spoken language can provide a powerful means of reinforcing or developing particular attitudes. The use of gender-dependent words should be avoided and we should use gender-neutral words particularly in relation to occupations, for example fire-fighter and police officer. Behaviour policies should make it clear that sexist language, which uses gender as a form of abuse, is inappropriate. A behaviour policy should be the same for both genders and crucially the same standards should be expected of each. Resources should be equally accessible to all learners and they should avoid the depiction of stereotypical roles. Resources should represent all sections of society and challenge prejudice, racism, sexism and injustice. It should be remembered that equality of opportunity applies to both genders. Boys can dominate the use of equipment in science, technology, design and computer studies and care should be taken to ensure that both genders receive equal hands-on experience. Both genders should have the same access to extracurricular and out-of-school activities. Single-sex competitions in sports are permitted only where physical differences between the sexes could disadvantage women or girls.

Sexual harassment is not defined in the Sex Discrimination Act, but it can be described as unwanted physical or verbal abuse of a sexual nature which adversely affects an individual. Bullying occurs when one person becomes a victim of another. This kind of bullying can arise from sexual stereotyping and is often based on the popular notions of 'acceptable' male or female behaviour. Importantly, it is unacceptable to discriminate on the basis of sexuality.

Ethnicity

Ethnicity can be a source of discrimination. There is an achievement gap between learners from different ethnic groups in the maintained sector. The 2001 Census shows that nearly one in eight pupils comes from a minority ethnic background and by 2010 the proportion is expected to be around one in five. In 2003 pupils in every ethnic group showed improvement in their GCSE/GNVQ results. However, pupils from a white ethnic background outperformed other ethnic groups. The problem is most severe for pupils from black Caribbean, black African, Pakistani and Bangladeshi backgrounds. Not all pupils from minority ethnic groups are outperformed by white pupils. Pupils from Indian and Chinese ethnic minority groups do significantly better than white pupils. We also need to be aware of the needs of gypsy/traveller children, asylum seekers/children of asylum seekers and pupils for whom English is an additional language. Where schools have high expectations and effective teaching and learning strategies underpinned by strong leadership, an inclusive ethos which demonstrates respect and does not tolerate racism and bad behaviour, then achievement for all pupils is high, irrespective of ethnicity. Discrimination can also be challenged where parents and the community play a full part in the life of the school.

Race

The Race Relations (Amendment) Act 2000 and the Code of Practice were introduced to enhance the existing framework for ensuring that all public authorities provide services in a way that is fair, accessible and non-discriminatory on the grounds of 'race', ethnicity or colour. The Amendment Act introduced three key changes to the Race Relations Act 1976. It widened and strengthened the anti-discrimination provisions to include all public functions. It extended the range and number of public authorities covered by the Act and it introduced a new and enforceable duty on key public authorities to promote race equality in all that they do. Educational organisations, as public bodies, need to promote equality of opportunity, good relations between persons of different racial groups and eliminate unlawful racial discrimination. They are required to have a race equality policy which covers staff, pupils, parents/carers and the wider community. This policy needs to be embedded throughout the organisation which has implications for the content of all policies and for the way in which they are implemented, monitored and reviewed.

Equality of learning

There is no single definition of this term; however, in the context of education, 'equal opportunities' can be taken to mean:

- Providing for all learners, regardless of gender, race, ethnicity, religion, disability etc.
- Being mindful of the difficulties that some groups can face and ensuring that any obstacles to them are removed.
- Being aware of personal prejudices and stereotypical views and avoiding labels related to these.
- Valuing each learner's worth.

Equality of opportunity is not the same as treating all people equally. We need to act to enable people to have equal access to opportunities, but it is their decision about which opportunities they pursue. For example, you could not listen to readers and apply the same criteria to all if some of the learners spoke English as a third language. In some cases positive action is necessary, sometimes referred to as 'positive discrimination', which involves changing the circumstances to one in which equality of opportunity can exist.

Task 12D

Consider your school. How far does it meet the requirements of the following acts?
Sex Discrimination Act 1975?
Race Relations Act 1976?
Equal Opportunities Legislation 1970?

Underachievement

The underachievement of a group or an individual can involve more than one factor. Individuals are members of many societal groupings. There have been various explanations for underachievement. Psychological (twentieth century) or Biological (nineteenth century) interpretations argue that there are natural differences between the sexes. Psychologists argued that some groups were simply more intelligent than others; therefore they did better in IQ tests and at school. However, the groups doing best in IQ tests were white, male and middle class. Other theorists argue that home background can account for underachievement. For some theorists schooling itself can lead to underachievement. Teachers can stereotype learners for example they may set lower expectations of those learners who are in the bottom streams in schools, the learners accepting this judgement and the labels attached to them thus developing anti-education sub-cultures. Material deprivation can also be argued to disadvantage certain groups. Halsey *et al.* (1997) set out to test the relative importance of cultural and material factors in a survey of the working class. He found that material factors were central to whether learners stayed on at school beyond the age of 16. A Marxist interpretation of this would argue that underachievement reflects wider social inequalities. Marxists agree that the curriculum affects pupils as it reflects the values of the ruling class. As a result, working class learners find themselves learning knowledge which they do not see as relevant and which is not based on what they already know. As a result, working class learners lack cultural capital and do less well in education.

Gender achievement

We have already identified inequalities in gender. Recent government initiatives have sought to eliminate gaps between all learners in terms of achievement. National Strategies have been designed to meet the needs of all learners through the promotion of active and independent learning. However, it is the underachievement of boys which is causing current concern. Girls now outperform boys in a number of subjects at GCSE level and this has generated what Epstein *et al.* (1998) refer to as a 'moral panic' about boys that is not limited to the UK, but also evident in many OECD countries. The gender gap is often accounted for by differences in maturity. Girls have more effective learning strategies at all ages and have responded well to equal opportunities programmes in schools and curricula which emphasise collaboration, talk and sharing. Whitehead (2002) has identified a 'crisis in masculinity'. Males are unsure of their role in relation to women. Some boys' choose to disregard authority, academic work and formal achievement, identifying with concepts of masculinity that can be seen as being in direct conflict with school ethos. Differences in learners' attitudes to work, goals and aspirations may be linked to wider social contexts, in particular the changing patterns of employment.

Underachieving schools

Under the current Ofsted Inspection framework schools can be judged to be 'underachieving'. In an underachieving school learners may achieve satisfactory levels in national tests. Closer examination of the school, however, makes it clear that pupils are not achieving as well as they could and should and that the school is achieving less than other schools in a similar situation. The judgement that a school is underachieving is based on performance data, rates of progress, concerns about expectations for learners, concerns about the nature of the curriculum including the level of challenge provided for different groups of learners and evidence that the school's trends of achievement and targets are too low. The ethos of the school can also be judged. If it is felt that the commitment to eradicating underachievement is not evident then a judgement can be made that the school is underachieving. It should be noted that the effects of such a label on staff is dramatic. Schools in such a position are likely to face some tough times. Nevertheless, they may come out of this period 'fighting', having had a chance to assess themselves and work out what they need to do to move forward.

Personalised learning

Personalised learning refers to the concept of providing education that meets individual needs, interests and aptitudes in order to ensure that every learner achieves the highest standards. The underpinning rationale is to raise standards by focusing learning and teaching on the aptitudes and interests of learners and by removing any barriers to learning.

> ... high expectations of every child, given practical form by high quality teaching based on a sound knowledge and understanding of each child's needs. It is not individualised learning where pupils sit alone. Nor is it pupils left to their own devices – which too often reinforces low aspirations. It means shaping teaching around the way different youngsters learn; it means taking the care to nurture the unique talents of every pupil.
>
> (Miliband 2004)

There are many benefits of personalised learning. Learners have their individual needs addressed. This can extend beyond the classroom, into the family and community with co-ordinated support. This should ensure that they are able to succeed to the full, irrespective of their talent or background. It also gives learners involvement and responsibility for their learning. Parents and carers can also receive regular information outlining what their child can currently do, how they can progress and what help they can give at home. They are involved in planning their children's future education and have an opportunity to play a more active role in school life knowing that their contribution is valued. This approach to planning for learning recognises the importance of placing the individual at the centre of any provision. It also recognises the impact that personal, moral and social education has upon the individual's development.

Personal, social and moral education

It is through socialisation and moral development that learners begin to create an understanding of who they are, developing a conscience and sense of morality. In this section of the chapter we look at some key theories in relation to the development of morality and the role of education in providing a curriculum that encourages the development of an individual's personal, social and moral growth. This will reflect some of the issues raised in Chapter 3.

Moral development

When we describe someone as having high moral standards we are referring to the standards of behaviour, fairness, honesty and so forth which they believe in. We are not referring to laws or other standards, although these may inform an individual's actions. Morality is a personal and/or social set of standards for behaviour. There have been several key theorists in this area.

Freud's psychoanalytic theory of moral development (1856–1939) is based upon a theory of 'identification', the process by which a child 'takes on' the attitudes and ideas of their parents. Children have an idea about 'good' behaviour. This is the ego ideal. They also have a concept of 'bad' behaviour which is developed by their conscience. Children must develop through each of Freud's psycho-sexual stages in order to achieve maturity. As explained in Chapter 3 the id is the original source of personality consisting of everything that is inherited including instinctive drives such as sex and aggression. It seeks immediate gratification. The ego develops out of the id because of the need to deal with the real world. It mediates between the demands of the id and the realities of the world. The superego is the internalised representation of the values and morals of society as taught to the child by society and parents. The id seeks pleasure, the ego tests reality and the superego strives for perfection. This view of moral development as a learned process is, however, problematic if we consider the issue of one-parent families where the child may not be able to 'identify' with an absent parent. We also have considerable evidence from Youth Offending Teams that children's moral behaviour is not fixed by the age of six or seven as Freud claimed. Children are far from reconciling their Oedipal dilemmas or achieving moral maturity.

Conditioning and social learning theory explores ways in which behaviours can be learned. It is in direct contrast to the Freudian view of identification. Piaget (1896–1980) proposed a sequence for moral development based on the stages of cognitive development. This is summarised in Figure 12.2, a sequence for moral development.

If we explore how children play games we can apply Piaget's framework for moral development At the age of two or three a pre-operational child will play a game with no rules demonstrating egocentric behaviour. By the age of four or five they are beginning to imitate rules and demonstrate moral behaviour in relation to the game. They are still mainly egocentric. Any rules children do follow are perceived as fixed. By the age of seven to eleven, children are obeying rules but not as slavishly as before. They can decentre.

Kohlberg (1986) developed Piaget's levels of cognitive development and divided them into six separate stages. He conducted his research based on responses to 'moral dilemmas', a dilemma being a problem which has two or more solutions, each of which is somehow wrong. His research led to the development of his levels of moral reasoning. Kohlberg

Figure 12.2 A sequence for moral development

Pre-moral	Up to age 4 approximately. No understanding of rules or right and wrong.
Moral realism	Between ages 4 and 9–10 approximately. Actions judged by material outcome. Rules come from authority (adults) and are fixed.
Moral subjectivism	From 9 or 10 Actions judged according to intentions. Rules are made by people but can be changed by agreement. Wrong is a transgression of moral principles.
Moral relativism	Puberty. The child decentres. Takes account of intention (autonomous morality) and motivation. Rules can be changed.

claimed that these different levels related to an individuals stage of cognitive development. See Figure 12.3.

However, if the stories presented to children are too complex then the outcome of Kohlberg's research studies may be flawed. The focus on 'reasoning' rather than on emotional aspects may also mean that the model is of limited application. As the research is based upon dilemmas it ignores the crucial elements of morality and can only claim to identify moral development in relation to wrongdoing.

PSHE/citizenship

Primary and Secondary schools provide for the emotional, physical and social needs of individual pupils through their pastoral care programmes. These should promote the school's values and should value individuals in their own right by creating a non-threatening atmosphere that encourages co-operation. Entitlement to PSHE and citizenship was established in the Education Act 1996 Section 456. PSHE covers a wide range of subjects including citizenship, drugs, alcohol and tobacco, emotional health and wellbeing, nutrition and physical activity (which is distinct from the physical education curriculum), finance,

Figure 12.3 Kohlberg's stage of cognitive development

Level	Stage	Characteristics
L1 Preconventional morality	1	Concern for outcome of behaviour. No conception of rules.
	2	Judged to be right if it satisfies own need. 'Right' gains reward.
L2 Conventional morality	3	Winning approval from others important .
	4	Child insists that there are rules which must be obeyed.
L3 Postconventional morality	5	Person holds a variety of values and opinions. Rules can be challenged.
	6	Level of deepest moral principles (rarely reached).

safety and sex and relationship education. PSHE encompasses all aspects of schools' planned provision to promote personal and social development, including health and well being. It is important that children and young people develop self-awareness, positive self-esteem and confidence in order to stay healthy and safe allowing them to engage in worthwhile and fulfilling relationships, whilst being able to respect differences between people and play an active role as members of society. It should also promote spiritual, moral, social and cultural development.

Lifelong learning

When do we begin the process of learning and when does learning end? It can be argued that even early child-play is the foundation for lifelong learning. The concept of lifelong learning is one that encompasses the view that we never stop learning and that we should access education and personal and professional development throughout our lives. Such learning can be formal or informal. In order that people can access education at any point in their life educational organisations such as colleges and universities are making access to their courses easier for 'non-traditional' entrants. That means that earlier formal requirements for qualifications to access further and higher education have been re-thought and a value has been placed on experiences within the workplace (formal or informal) or home. The delivery of educational programmes is becoming increasingly flexible as courses are offered at almost any point during the year and through virtual learning environments. Moreover, flexible attendance patterns and locations are offered.

Lifelong learning is diverse. It does not mean undertaking formal learning all the time. Learning is seen as an everyday activity that people will engage with throughout their life in order to update and acquire skills, knowledge and experience. This will enable all learners to adapt to changing employment needs and help meet the need for a workforce with higher-level skills. Links between learning and employment also mean that there should be a shared responsibility for lifelong learning between the state, employers and individual people.

Task 12E

Consider why primary and secondary schools should have an interest in promoting lifelong learning.

Schools should be encouraging a love of learning in pupils which can continue into adult life and as employers they also have an interest in encouraging and facilitating lifelong learning amongst their staff. There are many advantages in developing citizens who enjoy learning. The quest for learning can become contagious and build enthusiasms in people for particular subjects or topics. This is valuable in its own right as interested individuals transmit their zest for life. In addition, in a time where there are no 'jobs for life' it is increasingly helpful to be flexible and able to develop different skills and abilities at different periods in your life. As lifelong learners ourselves we as authors are enthusiasts about learning in all its forms.

Theorists' views of learning through play

Froebel (1782–1852) was a German educationalist who began the 'kindergarten' system. He emphasised the importance of play as a creative activity which helped children to realise their position in the world. He believed that learning environments required readily available materials and resources for exploratory play and that practical activities were central to learning. He sought to encourage unity, believing that people should be encouraged to be creative and productive whilst in harmony with religion and the world. He saw the purpose of education as being to:

> encourage and guide man as a conscious, thinking and perceiving being in such a way that he becomes a pure and perfect representation of that divine inner law through his own personal choice; education must show him the ways and meanings of attaining that goal.
>
> (Froebel 1896: 2)

Rudolph Steiner (1861–1925) saw community and individuality as opposing aspects of humanity. Every adult is made up of body, spirit and soul. He built 'schools of spiritual science', where the curriculum was based on 'spiritual insight' into the nature of children and how they learn. He believed that children went through 7-year stages from birth to 21. The key features of each stage are outlined in Figure 12.4.

Maria Montessori (1870–1952) was the first female doctor in Italy. She proposed an individual curriculum based on teacher assessments where children learn naturally in an appropriate learning environment. She believed that life skills such as washing hands and learning to dress were just as important as academic subjects. Children should be encouraged to become active learners and adult facilitators, with intrinsic rather than extrinsic motivation encouraged.

Figure 12.4 Key features of each stage of learning

Age	Characteristics
Birth to 7 years	The spirit comes to terms with being part of the material world Learning through imitation Learning of the alphabet, writing and reading Academic curriculum kept to minimum at this stage, exploration and play predominate
7–14 years	Characterised by imagination and fantasy The stage when children learn most effectively Children benefit from one teacher for whole of this stage to allow for community or family relationships to occur Children can emulate and accept authority and social roles Children interact with people and nature
14–21 years	The astral body is drawn into the physical body leading to puberty Creative subjects important but the use of ICT is discouraged

Susan Isaacs (1885–1948) promoted a progressive approach to education. She saw intellectual growth as closely linked to emotional development. This was secured through freedom in education which encourages learning and development of the self. Play was central to her desire to achieve educational freedom.

> The ultimate basis for the sensible practice of the trained educator ... provides a settled framework of control and routine, and definite help along social paths yet with ample personal freedoms ... this, too, is the corrective for the idea that the child will never learn unless he is scolded or smacked, no less than for the notion that he need not learn, but need only bring out the good in him.
>
> (Isaacs 1933:421)

Rubin *et al.* (1976) developed the first classification of play which outlined its function in social development. Play begins as a solitary activity developing into parallel play where children play individually but simultaneously. Looking-on play is the next phase where children engage in parallel play but begin to emulate the play of the other child. Joining-in play sees the first forays into communicating about the play activity. Co-operative play at the simple level sees children engaged with the process of joint play at a superficial level. At its most complex play becomes truly co-operative with all children taking an equal part in the direction and nature of the play activity.

There are problems with utilising play in the current educational system in the UK Play has a relatively low status which in turn makes it a low priority in the classroom. This is reflected in parental attitudes about reception children simply playing at school whereas in Year 1 the 'real' work begins. Provision for play in schools can also be poor and children may not have many play opportunities. Adults often don't understand their role in children's play. Play does not easily fit into an adult constructed curriculum because it happens holistically and across curriculum boundaries. It requires children to be in charge of their own learning which can be difficult to achieve in a school setting.

Conclusion

We began this chapter by identifying some of the aims of education which were linked to the role of education in society. We looked at the impact of ideology and culture on shaping our view of the aims of education and the impact of globalisation. At the beginning of the chapter you were asked to consider what you regarded as the aims of education. You may want to consider if you have revised these in light of your reading. We then moved on to look at the impact gender, ethnicity and race can have upon education and the role of the law in preventing discrimination. Issues of underachievement were discussed and recent developments in personalised learning were presented as a way of addressing underachievement issues for some pupils. The importance of personal, moral and social education was discussed in relation to providing a curriculum that meets the needs of all learners and we explored the important concept of lifelong learning and its basis in play and argued that there are some tensions between the current education system in the United Kingdom and the provision of play. The following list will provide you with some materials to follow up any of the issues raised in this chapter.

Bibliography

Blair, T. (1995) 'The power of the message', *New Statesman*, 29 September 2005: 20.

Bottery, M. (2004) *The Challenges of Educational Leadership: Values in a Globalized Age*, London: Paul Chapman Publishing.

Castells, M. (1998) 'End of the millennium. The information age', *Economy, Society and Culture*, 111. Malden, MA and Oxford: Blackwell.

2001 Census available at http://www.statistics.gov.uk/census/default.asp.

DTI (1999) *Economics of the Knowledge Driven Economy*, Conference Proceedings, London: Department of Trade and Industry.

Education Act 1996.

Epstein, D., Elwood, J., Hey, V. and Maw, J. (eds) (1998) *Failing Boys?* Buckingham: Open University Press.

European Commission (1999) *European Report on Quality Education: Indicators and Benchmarks of Quality of School Education*, Brussels: European Commisssion.

Froebel, F. (1885) *The Education of Man* (Translated by Hailmann, W.N.), New York and London: D. Appleton Century.

Froebel, F. (1887) *Letters on the Kindergarten* (Translated by Michaelis, E. and Moore, H.K.), London: Swan Sonnenschein.

Froebel, F. (1896) *Education by Development: The Second Part of the Pedagogics of the Kindergarden* (Translated by Jarvis, J.), New York: D. Appleton.

Froebel, F. (1900a) *Mother's Songs, Games and Stories* (Translated by Lord, F. and Lauder, E.), London: W. Rice.

Froebel, F. (1900b) *Pedagogics of the Kindergarten* (Translated by Jarvis, J.), London: Edward Arnold.

Halsey, A.H., Lauder, H., Brown, P. and Wells, A.S. (eds) (1997) *Education: Culture Economy, Society*, Oxford: Oxford University Press.

Hillman, J. and Stoll, L. (1994a) *Building Vision, Research Matters*, no. 2, School Improvement Network, London: Institute of Education.

Hillman, J. and Stoll, L. (1994b) *Understanding School Improvement, Research Matters*, no. 1, School Improvement Network, London: Institute of Education.

Isaacs, S. (1933) *Social Development in Young Children*, London: Routledge and Kegan Paul.

Kohlberg, L. (1986) *The Philosophy of Moral Development*, San Francisco, CA: Harper and Row.

MacBeath, J. (1999) *Schools Must Speak for Themselves: The Case for School Self-Evaluation*, London: Routledge.

Miliband, D. (2004) 'Personalised learning: building a new relationship with school', Speech at North of England Education Conference, Belfast; accessed at www.schoolsnetwork.org.uk/content/articles/1676/milibandlp.pdf July 2004.

Race Relations Act 1976.

Race Relations Amendment Act 2000.

Rubin, K.H., Maioni, T.L. and Hormung, M. (1976) 'Free-play behaviors in middle and lower class preschoolers: Parten and Piaget revisited', *Child Development*, 47, 414–19.

Sex Discrimination Act (SDA) 1975.

Whitehead, S. (2002) *Men and Masculinities*, Cambridge: Polity Press.

Appendix I

Record of task progress

Task	Notes and ideas	Product of work (if applicable)	Evaluations	Date to be revised (if applicable)
1A				
2A				
2B				
3A				
3B				
3C				
3D				
3E				
3F				
3G				
4A				
4B				

Task	Notes and ideas	Product of work (if applicable)	Evaluations	Date to be revised (if applicable)
4C				
4D				
5A				
5B				
5C				
5D				
6A				
6B				
6C				
6D				
7A				
7B				
7C				

Task	Notes and ideas	Product of work (if applicable)	Evaluations	Date to be revised (if applicable)
7D				
7E				
7F				
8A				
8B				
8C				
8D				
8E				
8F				
8G				
9A				
9B				
9C				

Task	Notes and ideas	Product of work (if applicable)	Evaluations	Date to be revised (if applicable)
9D				
9E				
10A				
10B				
11A				
11B				
11C				
11D				
12A				
12B				
12C				
12D				
12E				

Index

25 Tasks 11, 12
Abercrombie, K. 46
academic writing 6–7; and bibliographies 7–8;
     and referencing 6–7
Adams, M. 50
Additional Literacy Support (ALS) 118
Area Child Protection Committee 127, 128
Argyle, M. 46
Asperger's Syndrome 55, 102
assessment 2; and assessing learning 135–6;
     characteristics 136–7; definition 133;
     diagnostic/evaluative 133; e-assessment 140;
     and feedback 138–9; formative/summative
     133; Foundation Stage 135; of learning
     136; long-term 134–5; medium-term 134;
     methods for learners 138–9; motivation
     for 137; in National Curriculum 139–40;
     and peer/self-assessment 139; roles/
     responsibilities 140; short-term 134; and
     statutory National Curriculum tests 135;
     types 133–40
Assessment and Performance Unit (APU) 75–6
Assistant Special Needs Coordinator (Assistant
     SENCO) 11, 17, 118
Atkinson, M. 45
Attainment Targets (ATs) 79
attention deficit disorder (ADD) 100–1
attention deficit hyperactivity disorder (ADHD)
     100–1
augmentation communication systems (ACC)
     55
autism 101–2
Ayers, H. et al. 104, 106

Baddeley, G. 47
Bandura, A. 28
Barber, M. 5, 7
Barnes, D. 46, 47, 80
Basic Skills Agency 56–7
Bates, E. et al. 44
Baumrind, D. 22

Bee, H. 24, 27, 28, 38
behaviour management 2; attention deficit
     hyperactivity disorder 100–1; autism 101–3;
     behaviourist approaches 103–5; cognitive
     approaches 105–6; common forms of
     unwanted behaviour 97–101; discipline
     policies/procedures 107–8; emotional/
     behavioural difficulties 99–100; expected
     levels of behaviour 98; factors to consider
     98–9; psychodynamic/systemic approaches
     106–7; and self-esteem 108–9
Behaviourist approaches 103–4; Classical
     Conditioning 104; Operant Conditioning
     104; positive reinforcements 104; time outs
     104–5; token economy 104
Benton, A. 52
Bereiter, C. and Scardamalia, M. 56
Beynon, J. and Mackay, H. 88
Biggs, J.B. and Moore, P.J. 24, 29
Binns, R. 52
Boyes, M.C. and Allen, S.G. 22
the brain, and background music 37; brain
     buttons 35; cross crawl 35–6; development/
     language 35; effect of environment on 36–7;
     food 36; hook ups 36; physiology 34–5;
     strengthening 35–6
Breadth of Study 90
Brown, M. 60, 61
Bruner, J.S. 27, 43, 44–5, 47, 78
bullying 102–3, 127

Carr, R. et al. 23
Castells, M. 144
Chall, J. 50
Chambers, A. 48
child abuse, advice for children 126–7; child
     pornography 124; child prostitution 124;
     defining 123–5; domestic violence 124;
     emotional 124; fabrication of illness 125;
     female genital mutilation 124–5; forced
     marriage 124; neglect 124; physical 123;

responding to allegations/signs of 126; sexual 123; significant harm 125; suspected cases of 127, *see also* child protection
child development, cognitive theory 24–7; learning theories 27–9; motivation theories 29–32; psychoanalytical theory 23–4
child protection 2; designated teacher 128; legislation 122–3; procedures 127; register 125; and role of Teaching Assistants 128, *see also* child abuse
child rearing, authoritarian 22; authoritative 22; cultural differences 22; neglecting 22; parental or outside carers 22–3; permissive 22; practices/styles 21–3
Children Act (1989) 122–3, 139
Children Bill (2004) 128
Children's Learning in Science (CLS) 82
citizenship 153–4
Cognitive Acceleration through Science Education (CASE) 77
cognitive theory 24–7; assimilation, accommodation, adaption 24; and behaviour management 105–6; concrete-operational stage 25; formal-operational stage 26; pre-operational stage 25; and scaffolding 27; sensory-motor stage 25; and zone of proximal development 26–7
communication 45; barriers to 54–6; non-verbal 46; reading and writing 48–54; sign systems 55; speaking and listening 46–8; symbol systems 55
Continual Professional Development (CPD) 17–18; levels 18–19
Corden, R. 52, 56
Cover Supervisor 17
Curriculum Guidance for the Foundation Stage (2000) 90
Curtis, P. 12

Daily Mathematics Lesson (DML) 64–5
data management 93–4
Data Protection Act (1998) 139
Davis, R. 119
DeLaguna, G.A. 43
Department for Education and Employment 123
Department of Education and Skills (DfES) 79
design technology 83
differentiation 131
discipline policies/procedures 107–8
display assistants 17
Donaldson, M. 26, 78
drama 54
Driver, R. *et al.* 82
Dryden, G. and Vos, J. 26, 35–7, 78
dysarthria 55
dyscalculia 119–20

dyslexia 119
dyspraxia 55, 120–1

education, aims in 142; and equality of learning 149; and ethnicity 146, 148–9; and gender 146–7, 150–1; and globalisation 144–6; and ideology/culture 143–4; and learning through play 155–6; and lifelong learning 154; and moral development 152–3; and personalised learning 151; PSHE/citizenship 153–4; and race 9, 146; and sex discrimination 147–8; and society 143; and (under)achievement 150–1
Education Act (1981) 112
Education Act (1996) 153
Education Reform Act (1988) 79
Educational Psychologist 101
Emotional and Behavioural Difficulties (EBD) 99–100
emotional hijack 33
emotional intelligence 32
Epstein, D. *et al.* 150
Equal Pay Act (1975) 146
ethnicity 146–7, 148–9
Every Child Matters (2004) 128
Excellence and Enjoyment: A Strategy for Primary Schools (2003) 48

Five Year Strategy for Children and Learners (2004) 114
Foundation Degrees 12, 15, 18
Foundation Stage 79, 135
Fraser, H. and Honeyford, G. 72
Fredrickson, N. and Cline, T. 105, 106, 112
Freud, Sigmund 23–4, 152
Frith, U. 49
Froebel, F. 155

Gardner, H. 32, 38
gender 146–7, 150–1
Glasgow, K.L. *et al.* 22
globalisation 144–6
Goleman, D. 32
Goodman, K.S. 50, 54; and Goodman, Y.M. 57
Goswami, U. and Bryant, P.E. 51
Graduate Teacher Training Programme (GTTP) 18
Gregoire, M.A. 37
Gross, J. 31

Hallam, S., *et al.* 37; and Price, J. 37
Halsey, A.H. *et al.* 145, 150
Hancock, R. and Colloby, J. 9, 15
Harlen, W. 75
Hayhoe, M. and Parker, S. 51
health and safety 94

Health and Safety at Work Act (1974) 82
Higher Level Teaching Assistant (HLTA) 11,
    15, 18
Higher Level Teaching Assistant Standards 10,
    11
Hillman, J. and Stoll, L. 143
Hinds, D. 12
Holdaway, D. 54, 56
Howe, A. and Johnson, J. 53

inclusive education, Code of Practice 115–18;
    definition 112–14; and history of SEN
    111–12; mixed opinions concerning 114–15;
    and specific forms of SEN 118–21, see also
    Special Educational Needs (SEN)
Individual Behavioural Plan (BEP) 101
Individual Educational Plans (IEPs) 101, 112,
    116, 134
information and communication technology
    (ICT) 2, 14, 95–6, 145; critiques on
    teaching 88; definition 86–7; effective
    teaching/learning in 4–5; and group
    work 94; health and safety issues 94; and
    literacy 57; and managing data 93–4; and
    mathematics 71; and National Curriculum
    89–90; organisation/management of 92–3;
    planning for 90–1; progression/continuity in
    92; reasons for teaching 87–9; and science
    83; and supporting staff 93; and whole-class
    teaching 94
Information Technology (IT) 87
intelligence, emotional 32; emotional hijacks
    33–4; personal 32–3
Isaacs, Susan 156

Jenkinson, J. 112
Johnson, D.D., and Bauman, J.F. 51; and
    Johnson, R. 45
journals 6

Kagan, J. and Lang, C. 30
Kemmis, S. et al. 87
Key Stage 3 National Strategy 79
knowledge economy 144, 145
Knowledge, Skills and Understanding 90
Kohlberg, L. 152–3

language, behaviourist theory 43, 44; developing
    43–5; Initiation-Response-Feedback 44; and
    'private talk' 44; and role of talk 44–5; and
    science 80–1; social interactionist view 43–4;
    transmission/interpretation models 44; ways
    of communicating 45–54
learning, assessing 135–6; auditory 4;
    characteristics of assessment for 136–7; and
    ICT 94–5; kinaesthetic 4; location of study

4–5; and managing study time 4; objectives
    131; paradigms of 87–8; questioning 47; and
    reading 5–6; scaffolding 47; styles 3;
    visual 4
learning mentors 15, 17
learning theories 27; classical conditioning
    27–8; operant conditioning 28; social
    cognitive theory 28–9
LeDoux, Joseph 32
Lee, V. and Gupta, P.D. 26, 44, 51
Lefrançois, G.R. 29, 31
libraries 6
lifelong learning 154
Light, P. and Glachan, M. 45
List 99 (DEE) 123
listening 46–8
literacy 2; adult 56–7; and barriers to
    communication 54–6; and drama 54;
    environment 57–8; and ICT 57; and
    language 42–5; strategies supporting 56; ways
    of communicating 45–54
Literacy Hour 42–3
Local Education Authority (LEA) 117
LOGO 87
Lowey, 100
Lozanov, G. 37

MacBeath, J. 143
Maccoby, E.E. and Martin, J.A. 22
McGuire, J. and Richman, N. 23
Macintyre, C. 120; and McVitty, K. 120
Malloy, 46
Maslow, Abraham 31
mathematics see numeracy
Meek, M. 48, 51, 57
Melhuish, E.C. et al. 23
Mercer, N. 43
Merttens, R. 61
Miles, T.R. 119, 120
Millar, R. and Osborne, J. 74
Miliband, D. 151
Moderate Learning Difficulties (MLD) 115
Montessori, Maria 155
Montgomery, D. 104
moral development 152–3
Morgan, N. and Saxton, J. 81
motivation theories 29; cognitive 30–1;
    hierarchy of needs 31; humanist 31–2;
    physiological 29–30
music 37

National Agreement see Raising Standards and
    Tackling Workload: A National Agreement
National Association of Head Teachers
    (NAHT) 12
National College for School Leadership 89

National Curriculum (NC) 47, 57, 79, 87, 89–90, 135, 139–40
National Grid for Learning Programme (NGfL) 89, 92–3
National Literacy Strategy 42–3, 118, 135–6, 145–6
National Numeracy Strategy – Mathematical Vocabulary (1999) 66
National Numeracy Strategy (NNS) 63–7, 118, 135–6
National Remodelling Team 12, 14
National Standards for Teaching Assistants 10
National Union of Teachers (NUT) 11–12
National Vocational Qualifications (NVQs) 18
Neill, S. and Caswell, C. 46
non-verbal communication (NVC) 46
North, A.C. *et al.* 37
Nuffield Science Project 74
numeracy 2; at home/in the environment 71–2; definition 63–4; and developing curriculum 61–3; diagnostic assessment 67–9; formative assessment 67; and ICT 71; practical mathematics equipment 70; springboard group support material 70–1; strands 64; strategy 63–7; summative assessment 67; supporting mathematics 69–72; teaching/delivery techniques 62–3; understanding vs ignorance 61–2; unit plans 66; vocabulary 66–7; and Wave Intervention 69–70; whole-class interactive teaching 65

Open University Specialist Teaching Assistant Course (STAC) 11

Papert, Seymour 87
Pavlov, Ivan 27
personal intelligence 32; interpersonal 32–3; intrapersonal 32
personalised learning 151
Piaget, Jean 24–6, 45, 51, 76–8, 152
Pittman, L.D. and Chase-Lansdale, P.L. 22
planning 2; and assessment for learning 137; definition 130–1; types of 131–2
planning, preparation and assessment (PPA) 12
play 155–6
Pollock, J. *et al.* 119
positive discrimination 149
Post-Graduate Certificate in Education (PGCE) 18
programme of study (PoS) 79
Programme of Study for Speaking and Listening 47
psychoanalytic theory 23–4
psychodynamic theory 106–7

Qualifications and Curriculum Authority (QCA) 79, 90, 135

race 149
Race relations (Amendment) Act (200) 149
Raising Standards and Tackling Workload: A National Agreement (2003) 11–12, 13–14
reading 48–9; and alphabetic principle 50; apprenticeship approach 50; assessing 54; bottom-up models 49; guided/shared distinction 51; interactive models 50; phonic models 50–1; searchlight model 50; top-down models 49–50; using stories 52–3
Reardon, D.M. and Bell, G. 37
Reid, G. 119
remodelling programme 12, 14
Riches, C. 55
Roffey, S. and O'Reirdan, T. 108, 109
Rosen, M. 53
Rubin, K.H. *et al.* 156

Salovey, P., *et al.* 32; and Mayer, J. 33
SATs 133, 134
Savan, A. 37
Schemes of Work 79, 90–1, 132
School Change Team (SCT) 14
school links mentor 17
school science curriculum review (SSCR) 75
School Teachers' Pay and Conditions 12
science 2, 84; concepts 75; constructivist perspective 76–8; in the curriculum 79–80; and design technology 83; development of curriculum 74–8; ethical/moral dilemmas 78; and ICT 83; influence of Piaget on 76–8; and language 80–1; procedures 75–6; processes 75; and questioning 81–2; review of 74–5; safety in 82–3
Scott, T. 37
self-esteem 108–9
SEN (Special Educational Needs) Code of Practice (2001) 55, 69, 100, 118
sex discrimination 147–8
Sex Discrimination Act 148
Shayer, P. and Adey, M. 77
Skinner, B.F. 87
Soan, S. 112
speaking 46–8; exploratory stage 47; focusing stage 47; public stage 47; reorganising stage 47
Special Educational Needs Coordinators (SENCOs) 69, 118, 140
Special Educational Needs and Disability Act (2001) 114
Special Educational Needs (SEN) 2, 95, 134; and Code of Practice 115–18; definition 111; development of education for 112;

and gifted/talented learners 112; graduated
approach to process SEN children 117;
guidelines for 111; and identification/
school SEN register 115–16; and inclusive
education 112–15; and individual education
plans 116; and levels of support 116; and
SENCO/Assistant SENCO 118; and
statemented children 117; and targeting/
intervention 118, *see also* inclusive education
Specialist Teaching Assistant (STA) 11
specific learning difficulties (SpLD) 55
Springboard group support material 70–1
Springboard Mathematics 118
Stapleton, M. 29, 31
statemented children 117
Steiner, C. 32
Steiner, Rudolf 155
support staff 9
Sylva, K. and Lunt, I. 28
systemic approaches 106–7

Teachernet 15
Teaching Assistants, backgrounds 1; continual
professional development of 17–19; future of
15–17; management of 15, 16; role 2, 9–10;
skills 1–2, 3–8

Teaching Assistants (TAs), and planning
process 132
Trumper, R. 31

Vygotsky, L.S. 26–7, 44, 45, 78, 80

Wallace, S. 11, 17
Warnock Report (1978) 112
Waterland, L. 50
Wave Intervention 69–70
Wells, G. 45, 47, 48, 80
Westmacott, E.V.S. and Cameron, R.J. 103
Whitehead, S. 150
Wintgens, A. 55
Wood, D. 47
Woolnough, B. and Allsopp, T. 75
*Working with Teaching Assistants: A Good Practice
Guide* (2000) 15
World Wide Web (WWW) 89
Wray, D. and Medwell, J. 44
Wright, J.A. 55
writing 51–2; assessing 54; and audience/
function 52; shared 53–4; using stories 2–3

Youth Offending Teams 152